Sustainable Cities

Praise for this book

'The rich case studies in this volume offer new insight on the value of participatory action–research. What I found most valuable about the book was the variety of interventions presented and the recognition that empowering local communities is essential for the production of sustainable cities.'

Virginia Maclaren, Chair, Department of Geography and Program in Planning, University of Toronto.

'This publication takes the debate on sustainable urbanization beyond rhetoric. By engaging with a diverse number of initiatives in the urban Global South, the book offers great insights into the agency deployed by ordinary women and men, grassroots organizations, local governments, and NGOs in shaping environmentally sustainable and socially just urban futures.'

Adriana Allen, Senior Lecturer, Development Planning Unit (DPU), University College, London.

'This book is an excellent testimony of the necessary integration of disciplines and actors so as to achieve urban sustainability. It demonstrates how to reconcile research with action, local with global, and intangible with tangible urban environmental solutions. This book is proof that small-scale integrated and participatory solutions can improve urban living environments and reduce poverty.'

Oumar Cissé, Director of the Institut Africain de Gestion Urbaine (IAGU), Dakar.

'This book presents an original look at new approaches to try to meet one of the biggest challenges of the coming decades: the development and management of cities to ensure the sustainability of our planet.'

Alain Olivier, Professor of International Development, Université Laval, Canada.

Sustainable Cities
Local solutions in the Global South

Edited by Mélanie Robertson

PRACTICAL ACTION
Publishing

International Development Research Centre
Ottawa • Cairo • Dakar • Montevideo • Nairobi • New Delhi • Singapore

Practical Action Publishing Ltd
The Schumacher Centre
Bourton on Dunsmore, Rugby,
Warwickshire CV23 9QZ, UK
www.practicalactionpublishing.org

and the International Development Research Centre
P.O. Box 8500, Ottawa, ON K1G 3H9, Canada
www.idrc.ca/info@idrc.ca
ISBN (e-book) 978 1 55250 536 6

ISBN 978 1 85339 723 3

Since 1974, Practical Action Publishing (formerly Intermediate Technology
Publications and ITDG Publishing) has published and disseminated books
and information in support of international development work throughout
the world. Practical Action Publishing is a trading name of Practical Action
Publishing Ltd (Company Reg. No. 1159018), the wholly owned publishing
company of Practical Action. Practical Action Publishing trades only in support
of its parent charity objectives and any profits are covenanted back to Practical
Action (Charity Reg. No. 247257, Group VAT Registration No. 880 9924 76).

Cover design by Audrey François
Indexed by Liz Fawcett, Harrogate, North Yorkshire
Typeset in Stone Serif by Bookcraft Ltd, Stroud, Gloucestershire
Printed by Hobbs the Printers Ltd, Totton, Hamphire

Contents

List of illustrations

Figures

Photos

Tables

Box

List of acronyms and abbreviations

AAHDPO	Addis Ababa Housing Development Project Office
CBR	cost–benefit ratio
CCD	Commission Communale de Développement
CCDH-12	Centre Communautaire de Développement Humain
CDH	Centre pour le développement de l'horticulture
CEMI	Centre Misericordia
CLD	Comité Local de Développement
COPEMECO	Congolese Confederation Assisting Small and Medium Businesses
CTB	Coopération Technique Belge
Ecosan	ecological sanitation
EISMV	École Inter-États des Sciences et Médecine Vétérinaires de Dakar
GHP	Grand Housing Program
IAGU	Institut Africain de Gestion Urbaine
ICMSF	International Commission for Microbiological Speciations for Foods
IDRC	International Development Research Centre
IFAN	Institut Fondamental d'Afrique Noire
ILO	International Labour Organization
IRR	internal rate of return
MCA	multiple correspondence analysis
NGO	non-governmental organization
NHA	National Housing Authority
NPV	net present value
OR	odds ratio
OSWM	organic solid waste management
PUVeP	Peri-Urban Vegetable Project
REGIDESO	Régie de distribution d'eau
RRA	Rupnagar Residential Area
RRP	Rethink Reuse Project
SWOT	strengths, weaknesses, opportunities, and threats
UNEP	United Nations Environment Programme
USADEK	Union des jeunes Sages de Kisenso
WHO	World Health Organization

Preface

This book presents a selection of papers on research projects carried out by recipients of the ECOPOLIS Graduate Research and Design Awards – an initiative of the International Development Research Centre's (IDRC) Urban Poverty and Environment (UPE) programme, developed to help create and disseminate knowledge and innovation on themes related to the environment and poverty in cities. As a whole, the book provides practitioners engaged in policy development with a valuable reference source on a number of urban poverty and environment-related issues.

Between 2007 and 2010, the ECOPOLIS initiative issued awards to 27 master's and doctoral candidates undertaking innovative research or design projects in architecture, forestry, and other award categories. All of these projects integrated the development of tools and methods adapted to participatory research in urban settings, and all authors conducted a significant portion of their research on site.

The research papers featured in this book were among those presented at the workshop Envisioning ECOPOLIS — Innovations in Solving Urban Environmental Problems, held at the 2010 Congress of the Canadian Federation for the Humanities and Social Sciences, at Concordia University in Montreal, Canada. The workshop had two objectives: 1) to obtain an overview of the research of the ECOPOLIS award recipients and promote the dissemination of these works among academics, researchers, and policy-makers; and 2) to explore the opportunities and challenges associated with the practical application of research and present concrete means for tackling problems related to poverty and the environment in urban settings. Of the 27 ECOPOLIS award recipients, 15 had submitted proposals to a UPE call for papers to be presented at the workshop. Of those proposals, 14 were selected for presentation, and of those, in turn, 9 were selected for publication in this book. The final version of each paper integrates the viewpoints exchanged and the discussions held at the congress. Five of the nine papers were originally written in French and have been translated into English for this publication. The four other texts were written in English. All manuscripts were reviewed by experts from IDRC as well as by external evaluators.

I take this occasion to express sincere thanks to the many colleagues who contributed to the workshop, and thereby to the production of this book. Among these are, from IDRC's Climate Change and Water (CCW) programme, Mark Redwood (programme leader), Michele Leone (senior programme officer), and Matthew Watkins (summer student 2010), who assisted me in the review and selection of the texts. Moreover, from IDRC's Communications Division, Maria Brunelli advised the grant recipients on their oral presentation and Pauline Dole publicized the event. I also extend heartfelt thanks to CCW's Danielle Cantin for her contributions to ECOPOLIS and her support to the laureates. She provided invaluable assistance in the organization of the workshop and was involved throughout the event.

I furthermore wish to acknowledge the contributions of the researchers who supported the ECOPOLIS awards programme as external experts in the selection of the award recipients: Dr Adriana Allen (professor of urbanism at University College London, England), Dr Vikram Bhatt (professor of architecture at McGill University, Montreal), Dr Terrance Galvin (professor of architecture at Dalhousie University, Halifax), Dr Virginia MacLaren (professor of geography and urban planning at the University of Toronto), Dr Oumar Cissé (executive secretary, director of the Institut Africain de Gestion Urbaine, Dakar, Senegal), and Dr Denise Piché (professor of architecture at Université Laval, Quebec City).

I also wish to express sincere thanks to the people who contributed more directly to the production of this book: from IDRC, Rebecca McMillan (summer student 2011) and Luc Mougeot (senior programme officer); from Université Laval, Dr Denise Piché (professor of architecture), who accepted with no hesitation and on short notice to review the introduction and the conclusion of this book; and the translators and editors Cathleen Poehler and Anna Olivier, who ensured the quality of this book with dedication and professionalism. Lastly, my sincere thanks go to Bill Carman, from IDRC's Communications Division, who worked directly with me towards the realization of this book and who played a crucial role in communicating the importance and timeliness of such a work to the publishing house. He also ensured the follow-up of the extensive correspondence leading up to the publication of this book.

Finally, I am grateful to our English-language publishing house – Practical Action Publishing – for its commitment and efforts in giving these promising young researchers the opportunity to publish their research results in a well-illustrated, high-quality publication.

Mélanie Robertson
International Development Research Centre
Ottawa, Canada

About the editor

Mélanie Robertson is a senior programme officer at IDRC in Ottawa, Canada. She leads research projects on sustainable natural resource management in West Africa and Southern Africa, most of which focus on the use of geographic information systems in decision-making. She holds a PhD in geography from the Université de Montréal, Canada, and has also done post-doctoral research at the Institut Français d'Urbanisme of the Université de Paris VIII.

Introduction: The challenge of urban sustainability

Mélanie Robertson

Efforts by the international community to promote development and reduce poverty have traditionally concentrated on rural regions, thereby overlooking the urban factor. It was not until the turn of the third millennium that this imbalance was recognized, and then addressed through conferences, reports, and forums on urbanization and the state of the planet's cities. In the meantime, the global urban population crossed the 50 per cent threshold, making urbanization one of the most challenging issues facing humanity (UNPD, 2006). Although some reports highlight the opportunities presented by urban growth, most emphasize the difficult living conditions for the majority of urban inhabitants (UN-Habitat, 2006, 2007a), along with insecurity in all its forms (UN-Habitat, 2007b).

Concurrently, the drive towards sustainable development has given rise to different visions of a 'sustainable city'. Unfortunately, however, such visions rarely turn into reality, with interventions tending to be poorly adapted to their local contexts or lacking a sufficient grasp of the complex interrelations between the various dimensions of human insecurity, such as food, tenure, water, shelter, and health. Thus, realizing such visions calls for specific capacities and requires that researchers, policy-makers, and practitioners draw on the skills and knowledge of the communities themselves, as agents – and not merely victims – of urbanization. This book aims to provide a contribution to this effort.

Through nine case studies, the book addresses the diverse urban sustainability challenges facing cities in the Global South, such as tenure policy, water management, sustainable housing, waste treatment and recycling practices, urban agriculture, and construction practices. By featuring a dynamic mix of academic research and urban design projects from fields such as architecture, environmental science, agroforestry, anthropology, and urban planning, this book discusses the development of relevant tools and methods for conducting sustainable participatory research and practices in cities. The book thereby aims to promote sustainable, locally driven solutions devised by the populations and authorities who are struggling in the face of poverty.

This introductory section provides a brief overview of some of the key issues for integrated urban development. It begins by establishing the context of urbanization, poverty, and environmental degradation in the Global South at the beginning the 21st century, followed by a presentation of what I believe to be the most pressing challenge of urban sustainability, namely that of developing a more comprehensive and deeper understanding of what the notion of a 'sustainable city' really implies, and of the multi-faceted processes of change required to create such cities. This challenge and its associated issues are the common thread of the diverse case studies presented here and comprise the unifying theme of the volume.

Urban space in the Global South: The nature of urban poverty

The Global South is home to nearly three-quarters of the world's urban population and most of the world's largest and fastest-growing cities (UNPD, 2006). At its current pace, urbanization creates population densification, which exacerbates environmental and habitat-related problems of local, regional, and even global reach. The challenge to optimize resource use and waste generation in urban centres is thus of critical importance. In addition to environmental and habitat-related problems, urbanization is also characterized by poverty. The majority of urban dwellers live in shelters and neighbourhoods where they must contend with substandard conditions such as the following: poor-quality and overcrowded housing; inadequate water and food supplies; inadequate sanitation, drainage, and waste collection services; significant health challenges resulting from these conditions; difficulty getting healthcare and affording medication; difficulty keeping children in school; long working hours; and dangerous working conditions (Satterthwaite, 2003). The absence of services such as adequate water supply and sanitation services puts great pressure on the environment, as it leads to excessive groundwater pumping and accelerated soil and groundwater pollution (Uwejamomerea, 2011). Many tenants live in informal areas and are under the constant threat of being evicted, including by violent means. Moreover, the locations of these habitats are generally such that the impoverished urban populations are also more vulnerable to natural catastrophes such as droughts and floods. Those people occupying marginal land, floodplains, or riverbanks are vulnerable to flooding, while those living on slopes are at risk from landslides. Also, poorer groups are powerless within political systems and bureaucratic structures, leaving them little possibility of claiming support for developing their own initiatives (Mitlin and Satterthwaite, 2003). Of course, the scale and relative importance of these risks vary from person to person and place to place; however, large portions of urban populations in virtually all low- and middle-income nations face a mix of these deprivations (UN-Habitat, 2003).

This broader definition of urban poverty is key to understanding the environmental and habitat-related problems associated with poverty. Yet, the conventional quantitative methods for measuring urban poverty fail to incorporate this larger range of implications, focusing rather on income per se. However, a broader understanding of urban poverty is increasingly gaining ground (World Bank, 2001). Increasingly, research is focusing on how poverty can be mitigated in the face of stagnant incomes, either through improved services and infrastructure or through political changes that empower low-income groups (Satterthwaite, 2003).

In the same vein, the tendency to label many of the most pressing urban problems as strictly environmental and habitat-related is misleading. Doing so risks viewing these problems as 'natural', thereby overlooking the extent to which environmental problems are either exacerbated or mitigated by existing political, social, and economic structures. For example, inadequate access to resources does not necessarily result from a shortage of that resource per se. In the case of inadequate access to fresh water, limited access often results more from the government's inability or refusal to supply water to low-income areas (Hardoy et al., 2001). Even where resource shortages exist or where significant environmental change has taken place, the so-called environmental problems are usually exacerbated by political factors that prevent poorer groups from being able to access resources or services. For example, weather events such as floods will have a greater or lesser impact depending on the quality of local housing infrastructure, sanitation systems, or the early-warning and response systems in place. Thus, many environmental and habitat-related problems are also failures in governance, among them the failure to control pollution, limit occupational exposure, promote environmental health, provide basic infrastructure and services, allocate sufficient land for low-income housing developments, and counteract urban sprawl (Mitlin and Satterthwaite, 2003).

In search of the 'sustainable city'

The idea of 'sustainability' in many ways arose from the recognition of this more holistic view of poverty and environmental degradation. The *Brundtland Report*, issued in 1987, provided a first general definition of the concept: 'Sustainable development is development that meets the needs of the present without compromising the ability of future generations to meet their own needs' (United Nations, 1987: 43). Sustainable development is thus a much broader concept than environmental protection, encompassing as it does questions of inter- and intra-generational equity. Also inherent in the definition is the recognition that economic development must take place within the natural carrying capacity of the planet and be in harmony with other indicators of human well-being.

Drawing on the ideas of the *Brundtland Report*, the 'sustainable city' is a holistic system in which social, economic, environmental, and institutional aspects of development are mediated through urban design and are harmoniously integrated. Needless to say, this sustainable development agenda has raised new challenges for urban policy integration.

Local communities as well as national governments have since made commitments to turn urban areas into sustainable cities through various sustainable urban development and living practices. A veritable movement, this effort has engaged a multitude of actors, both at the theoretical and practical levels. Among these are professionals from the social, natural, and environmental sciences as well as engineers, each taking on specific tasks in the overall endeavour (Shmelev and Shmeleva, 2009; Williams, 2010). This has led to some remarkable results over the last three decades. In addition to the concrete improvements achieved by many projects, 'sustainability' is now a household word that figures in most policies. Nevertheless, this has not been able to prevent the exacerbation of urban problems, with cities and nations experiencing soaring poverty rates, rapid population growth, and dwindling resources.

As discussed, the problems faced by many cities (e.g. inadequate access to sanitation services, contaminated water supplies, inadequate waste management, and improper housing) run counter to sustainability efforts. For this reason, urban sustainability can hardly be claimed to have been meaningfully achieved. It appears that one cause of this failure results from the many diverging notions that researchers and practitioners have of 'sustainable cities', and further, of what the underlying notion of 'development' is. The various groups of actors engaged in urban sustainability have different approaches to and understandings of sustainability. Engineers, for example, prioritize efficiency and aim to quantify and map the availability of resources. Social scientists, for their part, emphasize social equity or justice, in particular as manifested in spatial settlement patterns (Williams, 2010). Yet, real progress in urban sustainability will require participants to adopt a more encompassing approach, namely one that considers the interplay of social factors together with scientific and technological solutions.

The research presented in this book challenges us to think more critically about the way we conceptualize and seek to realize the sustainable city. It also encourages us to embrace interdisciplinary perspectives rather than confining ourselves to a one-model-fits-all approach. These capacities are vital for developing more effective policies and practical solutions to specific problems. A broader dissemination of the debates across disciplines will also help achieve shifts within academic, practitioner, and public stakeholder groups, in turn leading to more radical paradigm shifts.

When trying to understand the 'sustainable cities' concept, we need to acknowledge the powerful trends at work across different countries, as well as the remarkable spatial and cultural diversity among the efforts to pursue this goal. For example, sustainability efforts in Dakar are generally different from those in Bangkok. Furthermore, while this book focuses particularly on the Global South, it is important to not underestimate the urgency of challenges in the Global North. In the Global North, as in the Global South, it is low-income and socially excluded populations who are most directly impacted by habitat-related environmental problems. Indeed, urban 'environmental justice' movements in the North have highlighted the ways in which environmental burdens are unequally distributed across lines of income, race, and gender.

Nevertheless, by and large Northern societies can be said to face fewer environmental challenges, mainly due to the fact that Northern economies 'export' many of these challenges, thereby externalizing adversities and reaping profits. For example, the more environmentally and socially irresponsible stages of industrial production processes have been outsourced to the Global South, which has more lenient legal frameworks and policies and little leverage in international trade negotiations.

Thus, the sustainability challenges in the North and South are distinct but interlinked. The North is arguably the biggest contributor to the world's environmental problems due to its overconsumption of resources, while the environmental problems of the people in the Global South often result from their inadequate access to resources. This is largely due to the historically disadvantaged position of the Global South, which is further exacerbated by local factors.

These different challenges across local contexts as well as the North–South divide must be acknowledged in efforts to achieve sustainability. However, this does not preclude the potential for the transfer of knowledge and experiences across contexts, including from the South to the North.

Small-scale interventions for better city living

This book provides a space to explore different perspectives and to discuss the possibilities for small-scale and integrated solutions to the core challenges of sustainable development. The featured case studies comprise small-scale interventions and technological innovations, which are arguably the only pathway to change available in the Global South. The solutions proposed here could potentially be transferred to the North. Indeed, urban infrastructures in the North, for example wastewater recycling systems, are in many cases outdated and inefficient.

In its action-oriented approach, this book contributes to a wider body of local-level participatory action research supported largely by international development agencies. Out of this research, two important conceptual frameworks have emerged: the 'urban livelihoods' approach, promoted by the Department for International Development of the UK (Rakodi and Lloyd-Jones, 2002); and the city development strategies promoted by the Cities Alliance. These frameworks address specific challenges such as slum upgrading and other issues concerning land tenure regulation (UN-Habitat, 2005a; Greene and Rojas, 2008).

Similarly, Jenkins et al. (2007) show that in order to develop adaptive and efficient local solutions to the urban problems of cities undergoing accelerated development, policies and approaches regarding housing, land, and urbanism must be better anchored in tradition, culture, and local customs (UN-Habitat, 2003; Vélez-Guerra, 2004; Du Plessis, 2005; Fitzpatrick, 2005; Muller-Friedman, 2005; Chauveau et al., 2006; Nkurunziza, 2008). These authors even postulate that urban planning can be adapted to land regimes and that statutory land tenure regimes are a condition of good governance.

However, despite their growing acceptance in academia, these conceptual frameworks remain largely unexploited in the field. Furthermore, while these two approaches place great emphasis on land development, they fail to examine the spatial and physical organization of the immediate living environment, treating this important factor as though it were simply the result of other domains of intervention. Indeed, there is a general lack of research in the Global South on the structures and forms to be given to nature and the built form such that these can co-exist in harmony (Allen, 2003; Bâ, 2005; Fall and Gueye, 2005; McGregor et al., 2006).

Some scholars are exceptional in this regard. We can highlight, for example the works of Habraken (1998) and those of the Global Urban Research Unit of Newcastle University, in particular those of Kellett and Tipple (2005), focus on the integration of remunerating activities into the living environment and on the ways in which inhabitants can transform their surroundings.

This book joins these pioneering scholars in emphasizing the appropriate form, or spatial organization, for different types of land usage. Specifically, the studies presented in this book are part of a growing research trend in which human establishments are considered as part of nature (Calthorpe, 2001; Hough, 2004). Thus rather than adhering to a strict dichotomy between the natural and built environments, and likewise between structure and lifestyle/practice, the chapters in this book adopt implicitly or explicitly the broader notion of 'habitat'.

Through this lens, the authors in this book seek small changes in practice and structure, which can create more balanced, healthy, and sustainable habitats. These solutions confront six interconnected challenges to urban sustainability, which are reflected in the six themes of this volume.

The emergence of a collective work: Nine solutions for improving urban and peri-urban living environments

The case studies in this book revolve around six interconnected themes: urban agriculture, construction practices, the co-existence of formal and informal systems, housing and land tenure, water management, and waste treatment and recycling. Representing cities in Sub-Saharan Africa (Senegal, Ethiopia, Congo), Asia (Philippines, Thailand, Bangladesh), and Latin America (Peru), they present a set of reflections along with possible solutions that are both locally adapted and globally relevant.

1 Urban agriculture: An essential key in the fight for food security?

In cities, poverty and food insecurity are directly related. Disadvantaged city dwellers depend more on money than do their counterparts in rural environments, as almost all their daily essentials must be purchased with money rather than foraged, cultivated, or traded. This makes urban residents highly vulnerable to food price increases. In fact, one of the main causes of food insecurity lies in the high cost of food in relation to income. While most rural inhabitants can cultivate a lot of land, city dwellers must buy most of the food they consume. The latter applies less so if they receive food donations or other forms of food aid from family, friends, or rural kin. However, in recent decades increasing numbers of urban dwellers have been growing food for their own consumption, thereby achieving significant savings and income, which they then apply to buying other food or to cover other household expenses. In this way, urban agriculture has become one of the main survival strategies of the most disadvantaged urban populations. Therefore, when urban agriculture is integrated into the urban planning process and the habitat, it has the potential to generate resources and benefits (Mougeot, 2005). Among these are the reduction of the vulnerability of poor urban households, enhancing the health of the individual and the rehabilitation of poor neighbourhoods, in that urban agriculture builds a healthy and sustainable urban environment. Urban agriculture is also the driving motor for the development of participatory local governance, chiefly because its practice is open to all social groups and because it stimulates modes of collective management. Lastly, as urban agriculture is often a female activity, it allows women to ensure the survival of their families. In many cases, urban agriculture even provides women with a source of income, thereby allowing them to secure their independence and leave poverty behind. Urban agriculture in the Global South has recently become the object of increasing research (Koc et al., 2000; Mougeot, 2006; Redwood, 2009), in particular with regard to the constraints and risks it faces, which, if unattended, threaten to derail its contribution to more sustainable cities (Mougeot, 2006). The question is thus whether and how livestock production and market gardening can be made more accessible, safer, and more productive while allowing for the inevitable densification linked with urbanization.

A key challenge is planning multi-functional spaces at both the neighbourhood and household levels. In this book, Mariève Lafontaine-Messier demonstrates how neighbourhoods can harness urban green spaces for both leisure and productive purposes. Her study explores the implementation of food-producing trees in public parks of a neighbourhood in Villa El Salvador, located in the metropolitan region of Lima, Peru. By allowing for food production in urban settings, such systems can contribute to combating food insecurity while allowing residents to benefit from the environmental services provided by trees. Such systems also circumvent the problem of land tenure conflicts that usually exists between developers and those practising urban agriculture. The project's success can also be attributed to its recognition of the importance of taking into account local traditions and customs when attempting to improve subsistence conditions. The studies by Émilie Pinard and Jessica Gagnon, for their part (to be outlined in more detail in the next sub-section) show how appropriate construction practices developed in partnership with communities can integrate agriculture and livestock breeding into the living and working environments in ways that minimize health risks and public disturbance.

2 The importance of good construction practices

The design and development of living environments promote the creation of productive communities in general. This is partly because the construction industry is a large employer in the Global South, as it is everywhere in the world (Lawrence et al., 2008). At the same time, the built environment is also increasingly recognized as an important factor in people's health and quality of life. The quest to improve building techniques and materials has led to many experiments, and the environmental performance of buildings has been extensively studied in both local settings and in the context of technologically sophisticated architecture. UN-Habitat, for example, published a thorough review of the works realized by and for the Global South on this topic (2005b). It concluded that most research is focused on developing a better understanding of the lifestyles and construction practices in informal settings, namely with the goal of improving existing practices. This approach appears to have had more success than the introduction of new technologies or new housing models. For some time now, locations are being transformed, through participatory means, into testing and training grounds, either to facilitate horticultural and livestock production, to optimize on-site treatment of water and waste, or to improve building practices by using waste materials. These approaches are accessible to the people directly involved in building (e.g. small builders, masons, day labourers – often youth) as well as to the households themselves. Emphasis is placed on resources, knowledge, and local know-how.

The studies by Pinard and Gagnon insist on the role of the built environment in the improvement of production capacities. Their suggestions for redesigning the built environment emphasize the generation of productive activities. Their studies, both based in Malika, a suburb of Dakar, also develop participatory intervention measures that make use of research on livestock breeding and the market-gardening culture. The action research of Pinard, conducted at a women's centre, shows how architecture can become a catalyst for the participation of women in local governance and ecological practices. It offers possible solutions for ensuring the spread and dissemination of acquired skills, in particular regarding the reduction of environmental and sanitary degradation. Specifically, Pinard calls for an eco-systemic approach when developing housing compounds and neighbourhoods, the improvement of construction techniques, and the creation of local training programmes based on learning in action. Her project activities provided women and municipal stakeholders with opportunities to determine, adapt to, and evaluate technical and social innovations designed to improve their living conditions. The research by Gagnon supports domestic pig breeders in improving their living conditions and livestock breeding techniques through the identification of and experimentation with small structural modifications that reduce the sanitary and environmental risks to their households. These structural modifications focus on the better management and handling of pig manure, the reduction of the physical burden of livestock breeding tasks, and the promotion of ergonomic improvements to existing sanitary practices.

While Pinard demonstrates that design can foster participation and cooperation, the chapter by Ejigu illustrates that inappropriate planning and design can reduce quality of life and inhibit the development of community. His chapter explores a government programme for co-ownership and low-cost housing construction in Addis Ababa, Ethiopia, examining in particular how the programme's standardized condominium blocks discourage traditional social and productive activities. For example, inhabitants were assigned to their new dwellings irrespectively of former relations with neighbours from their initial communities. The isolated nature of the units further discouraged interaction between neighbours, who often competed for use of the limited public space. On the whole, this gap between the physical form of the housing and the mode of life weakened overall community cohesion. The inhabitants were also ostracized by community members outside of the condominium complex. Not surprisingly, many residents ended up rejecting these housing arrangements.

3 Building links between formal and informal sectors

The case study by Ejigu reveals a tension inherent in urban development in the Global South, namely, the incompatibility between formal and informal systems. Despite the fact that informal urban growth is increasingly recognized as a driving force and has become the object of diverse studies, the links between formal and informal systems remain tenuous (Champion and Hugo, 2004; Neuwirth, 2006). The increasing focus on informal settlements has been partially fuelled by a growing awareness of the fact that the sustainable development of cities is highly dependent on the way in which urban, agricultural, and natural settings co-exist there (Tacoli, 2007). As a result, any sustainable urban development effort must begin by strengthening links between the formal and informal sectors. In addition, efforts must be made to improve the understanding of those links and their significance. The study by Kamathe Katsongo attempts to fill this research gap. His study explores the challenge of building links between the formal and informal sectors through an examination of partnership modalities for managing drinking water. His case study of a neighbourhood of Kinshasa, Congo, compares different solutions that have been implemented by public actors and informal collective operators. He observes that the interactions between participants in the formal drinking water management system and the other actors are characterized more by rivalry than by cooperation. However, certain partnership modalities were shown to have potential if they could be formalized and made more self-sufficient. He moreover emphasizes that partnerships between the public actors and informal collective operators are very difficult to establish in the absence of a solidarity-based socio-political environment. Even when government policies are favourable and when appropriate decentralization exists, resources and governance mechanisms are rarely sufficient to establish a partnership with the informal sector and the disadvantaged communities. As a result, proclaimed policy goals often remain dead letters. In fact, the public policies and methods of local administrations and national governments often tend to discourage rather than support the efforts and investments of disadvantaged urban communities. Consequently, adaptation strategies typically fall outside of the legal framework.

4 Housing and land tenure insecurity: An exacerbating factor

The problem of political and social marginalization of informal communities is compounded by the complexity of land tenure issues in 'informal' zones, which are largely unregulated and sometimes not even displayed on municipal official maps. Tenure insecurity is one of the underlying causes of the suboptimal use of natural resources, exerting undue pressure on the environment. Abrupt increases in land prices, due to rapid demographic growth, are also a major obstacle in providing adequate housing. Urban planning usually caters to the most lucrative housing markets, often leaving even the middle class with insufficient viable land (Everett, 1999). In fact, the price of viable land in the Global South cities is sometimes as high as the same kind of land in industrialized countries, where income per inhabitant is normally much higher. New migrants and the impoverished inhabitants of cities, who have limited financial means and inadequate access to loans, therefore have no choice but to settle on marginal land, usually as illegal occupants of vacant land or with an otherwise questionable legal status (Alder, 1995). Impoverished populations generally do not have the legal right to occupy vacant land, and governments generally fail to adopt laws or policies authorizing its use or recognizing the right of usage, which is distinct from tenure rights. The impossibility of making themselves heard or of exerting influence at the political level leaves disadvantaged city dwellers with little recourse. In the absence of property titles, or in cases when titles are poorly established or contestable, the cities cannot allocate land or loans to inhabitants to launch profitable productive activities, and often public services refuse to supply non-regularized areas.

Governments generally do not intervene in the real-estate market when attempting to provide low-income housing in proximity to income-generating activities to the urban poor. And when they do, the actual needs of this population group are not necessarily given sufficient consideration. Ejigu's study on low-income housing in Addis Ababa, Ethiopia, for example, suggests that the government may have been driven more by a desire to 'modernize' the city than by the need to provide functional and high-quality housing for the urban poor. Correspondingly, the constructed condominium units proved less suitable for the urban poor. Also, in many cases the potential revenue to be gained by renting out their acquired housing units prompted many condominium owners and their families to continue living in more disadvantaged, precarious areas while using the rental income to cover household expenditures such as healthcare and school fees.

As a whole, the studies found that an absence of affordable and appropriate rental housing in the formal economy promotes the proliferation of informal construction. The study by Mohamed Kamruzzaman, for example, examines common practices in informal housing construction in Dhaka, Bangladesh. He discusses the 'piecemeal' construction practice typical of the informal housing sector whereby developers gradually erect apartment buildings bit by bit as they acquire the capital to expand their units. Kamruzzaman moreover explains that government interventions in Bangladesh, as elsewhere, to provide low-cost housing generally fail to integrate or give credit to informal construction efforts, despite the significant degree to which this sector contributes to compensating for a shortcoming of the formal sector. It should be mentioned, however, that some public housing programmes have in fact integrated the gradual approach to house building as practised in the informal sector, mainly by providing basic shelter units that can then be expanded and improved. Kamruzzaman concludes that government housing programmes would be more effective if they engaged the existing informal sector.

5 Access to clean water: A public health concern

As with housing, the informal sector has also been forced to fill gaps in the formal water and sanitation systems. Most specialists agree that access to clean water is one of the main challenges facing humanity today (Satterthwaite, 1995, 2003). In fact, only a very small proportion of city dwellers living in poor urban zones have access to clean water. In general, public water networks benefit mainly the middle and upper classes. Most informal neighbourhoods of the Global South have neither a wastewater treatment system nor connection to the water supply network.

As Katsongo demonstrates, household water supply to the urban poor, mostly managed by private vendors, is generally inadequate in the sense that it is irregular and unpredictable, of varying qualities, and extremely expensive. Thus, not only are the urban poor burdened with major expenditures, they are also exposed to elevated health risks (Ruel et al., 1999).

The case study by Mamadou Ndiaye focuses on these health impacts. His study examines the health risks associated with the use of wastewater in urban agriculture for riparian communities in Dakar, Senegal. In Senegal, farmers often prefer to use wastewater to irrigate their fields, as it is more accessible and reduces the need for fertilizers. Although this practice is technically banned in Senegal, authorities typically turn a blind eye rather than collaborating with farmers to find acceptable solutions. However, possibilities for collaboration do exist, such as the identification of alternative parcels of land where sources of fresh water would allow for irrigation, the building of inexpensive and viable purification stations, or the development of a full range of solutions for reducing the risks of using untreated water.

Even minor improvements in living and construction practices could make an important difference. As many of the case studies in this book illustrate, the need for the collection and treatment of water and wastewater has inspired small improvements to the built environment.

For example, the case study by Pinard shows how a wastewater management system was integrated into the design of a women's centre, which improved the quality of the immediate environment and served to raise awareness among the women about the importance of water management. However, much research is still required with regard to the implementation of such systems, and in particular systems for separating greywater from blackwater, within domestic spaces and neighbourhoods, and the evaluation of their performance.

6 Promotion of waste treatment and recycling practices

Waste treatment is another major problem for most communities in the Global South. The massive, uncontrolled disposal of diverse forms of untreated waste has harmful consequences for the environment and residents. The inadequacy and irregularity of official collection leads to the proliferation of anarchic deposits of household waste, which are sources of odour and infection, in addition to constituting 'visual pollution'. The management of household waste, although usually declared a priority within municipal waste treatment programmes, is generally limited to isolated approaches that are not viable over the long term. Yet, while an environmental burden, waste does in fact offer the potential to generate productive activities when considered from the angle of reclamation. In the last chapters of this book, Diana Guerra and Jeannette M. E. Tramhel discuss waste management, a topic essential to the Global South, in their efforts to overcome environmental problems. Both authors consider waste as a productive resource and try to find ways of drawing benefit from it. The action research by Guerra focuses on the reuse of waste in Koh Kred, Thailand, as a means to generate income for people whose lives are marked by instability. Guerra provided participants with the skills, tools, and information necessary for helping the local community maintain a long-term waste separation programme that integrates waste reuse as a daily activity and that generates income while improving the environment. The study by Tramhel focuses on the integration of organic waste management into urban agriculture in Cagayan de Oro, Philippines. Her research seeks to improve community solutions for the use of waste as an agricultural input. Both of these projects underline that the built environment can be redesigned to promote a closing of resource loops at municipal or district levels through waste collection and recycling systems that are more accessible, more affordable, and easier to manage than those implemented in developed countries.

The studies featured in this book build on the premise that the spatial organization of the habitat and the built environment, compounds, and neighbourhoods has a major impact on the health of people and the environment, including the conservation of resources. They engage in an exploration to find small-scale solutions for improving urban and peri-urban living environments, founded on the sharing of knowledge among all stakeholders, the development of a collective vision, and the empowerment of communities to take charge of their territories. Emphasis is placed on developing and implementing a participatory approach to improving living conditions that targets the reduction of poverty while contributing to the rehabilitation and protection of the habitat and the environment.

References

Alder, G. (1995) 'Tackling poverty in Nairobi's informal settlements: Developing an institutional strategy', *Environment and Urbanization* 7(2): 85–107.

Allen, A. (2003) 'Environmental planning and management of the peri-urban interface: Perspectives on an emerging field', *Environment and Urbanization* 15(1): 135–47.

Bâ, C. (2005) 'Du concept d'approvisionnement à un point de vue géographique sur les relations villes/campagnes en Afrique au Sud du Sahara' in A. S. Fall and C. Gueye (eds) (2005) *Urbain-rural: l'hybridation en marche*, pp. 355–70, ENDA Tiers-monde, Dakar.

Calthorpe, P. (2001) *The Regional City: Planning for the End of Sprawl*, Island Press, Washington DC.

Champion, T. and Hugo, G. (eds) (2004) *New Forms of Urbanization: Beyond the Urban Rural Dichotomy*, Ashgate, Aldershot, Hants and Burlington, VT.

Chauveau, J.-P., Colin, J.-P., Jacob, J.-P., Lavigne Delville, P., and Le Meur, P.-Y. (2006) *Modes d'accès à la terre, marchés fonciers, gouvernance et politiques foncières en Afrique de l'Ouest*, IIED, London.

Du Plessis, J. (2005) 'The growing problem of forced evictions and the crucial importance of community-based, locally appropriate alternatives', *Environment and Urbanization* 17(1): 123–34.

Everett, M. (1999) 'Evictions and human rights: An ethnographic study of development and land disputes in Bogotá, Colombia', Lincoln Institute of Land Policy, Cambridge.

Fall, A. S. and Gueye, C. (eds) (2005) *Urbain-Rural: l'hybridation en marche*, ENDA Tiers Monde, Dakar.

Fitzpatrick, D. (2005) '"Best Practice" options for the legal recognition of customary tenure', *Development and Change* 36(3): 449–75.

Greene, M. and Rojas, E. (2008) 'Incremental construction: A strategy to facilitate access to housing', *Environment and Urbanization* 20(1): 89–108.

Habraken, N. J. (1998) *The Structure of the Ordinary. Form and Control in the Built Environment*, MIT Press, Cambridge, MA.

Hardoy, J. E., Mitlin, D., and Satterthwaite, D. (2001) *Environmental Problems in Cities of Africa, Asia and Latin America*, Earthscan, London.

Hough, M. (2004) *Cities and Natural Process: A Basis for Sustainability*, Routledge, London.

Jenkins, P., Smith, H., and Wang, Y. P. (2007) *Planning and Housing in the Rapidly Urbanising World*, Routledge, London.

Kellett, P. and Tipple, A. G. (2005) 'Researching domestic space and income generation in developing cities' in D. U. Vestro, Y. Hurol, and N. Wilkinson (eds) *Methodologies in Housing Research*, pp. 204–21, Urban International Press, London.

Koc, M., MacRae, R., Mougeot, L. J. A., and Welsh, J. (eds) (2000) *Armer les villes contre la faim. Systèmes alimentaires urbains durables*, International Development Research Centre, Ottawa.

Lawrence, R. J., Gil, M. P., Flückiger, Y., Lambert, C., and Werna, E. (2008) 'Promoting decent work in the construction sector: The role of local authorities', *Habitat International* 32(2): 160–71.

McGregor, D., Simon, D., and Thompson, D. (eds) (2006) *The Peri-Urban Interface. Approaches to Sustainable Natural and Human Resource Use*, Earthscan, London.

Mitlin, D. and Satterthwaite, D. (eds) (2003) *Responding to Squatter Citizens: The Role of Local Governments and Civil Society in Reducing Urban Poverty*, Earthscan, London.

Mougeot, L. J. A. (ed.) (2005) *Agropolis. The Social, Political, and Environmental Dimensions of Urban Agriculture*, International Development Research Centre, Ottawa.

Mougeot, L. J. A. (2006) *Cultiver de meilleures villes. Agriculture urbaine et développement Durable*, International Development Research Centre, Ottawa.

Muller-Friedman, F. (2005) '"Just build it modern": Post-Apartheid spaces on Namibia's urban frontier', in S. J. Salm and T. Falola (eds) *African Urban Spaces in Historical Perspective*, pp. 48–71, University of Rochester Press, Rochester, New York.

Neuwirth, R. (2006) *Shadow Cities: A Billion Squatters, A New Urban World*, Routledge, London.

Nkurunziza, E. (2008) 'Understanding informal urban land access processes from a legal pluralist perspective: The case of Kampala, Uganda', *Habitat International* 32(1): 109–20.

Ruel, M., Haddad, L., and Garret, J. (1999) 'Some urban facts of life: Implications for research and policy', *World Development* 27(11): 1917–38.

Rakodi, C. and Lloyd-Jones, T. (eds) (2002) *Urban Livelihoods. A People-Centred Approach to Reducing Poverty*, Earthscan, London.

Redwood, M. (eds) (2009) *Agriculture in Urban Planning. Generating Livelihoods and Food Security*, Earthscan, London.

Satterthwaite, D. (1995) 'The underestimation of poverty and its health consequences', *Third World Planning* 17(4): 3–12.

Satterthwaite, D. (2003), 'The links between poverty and the environment in urban areas of Africa, Asia, and Latin America', *Annals of the American Academy of Political and Social Science*, 590: 73–92.

Shmelev, E. S. and Shmeleva, I. A., (2009) 'Sustainable cities: Problems of integrated interdisciplinary research', *International Journal of Sustainable Development* 12(1): 4–23.

Tacoli, C. (ed.) (2007) *The Earthscan Reader in Rural–Urban Linkages*, Earthscan, London.

UN-Habitat (2003) *The Challenge of Slums: Global Report on Human Settlements 2003*, Earthscan, London.

UN-Habitat (2005a) *Enabling Shelter Strategies: Review of Experience from Two Decades of Implementation*, UN-Habitat, Nairobi.

UN-Habitat (2005b) *Building Materials and Construction Technologies: Annotated UN HABITAT Bibliography*, UN-Habitat, Nairobi.

UN-Habitat (2006) *State of the World's Cities 2006/2007*, UN-Habitat, Nairobi.

UN-Habitat (2007a) *Droits des femmes au sol, à la propriété et au logement: Guide global pour les politiques publiques*, UN-Habitat, Nairobi.

UN-Habitat (2007b) *Enhancing Urban Safety and Security: Global Report on Human Settlements 2007*, UN-Habitat, Nairobi.

United Nations (1987) *Brundtland Report*, Report of the World Commission on Environment and Development, General Assembly Resolution 42/187, United Nations, New York.

UNPD (United Nations Population Division) (2006) *World Urbanization Prospects: The 2005 Revision*, United Nations, New York.

Uwejamomerea, T. (2011) 'The challenge of urban poverty and inequalities in developing world cities: Issues and options for the sanitation and water sector', *International Journal of Urban Sustainable Development* 1(3): 127–31

Vélez-Guerra, A. (2004) *Multiple Means of Access to Land for Urban Agriculture: A Case Study of Farmers Groups in Bamako, Mali*, Cities Feeding People Report Series, Cities Feeding People program initiatives, International Development Research Centre (IDRC), Ottawa.

Williams, K. (2010) 'Sustainable cities: Research and practice challenges', *International Journal of Urban Sustainable Development* 1(1–2): 128–32.

World Bank (2001) *World Development Report 2000/2001: Attacking Poverty*, Oxford University Press, Oxford.

Chapter 1

Food-producing trees in urban public spaces: An innovative strategy to fight poverty in Villa El Salvador, Peru

Mariève Lafontaine-Messier

Abstract

This action-research project examined the feasibility and viability of integrating food-producing trees in urban forestry as a means to combat food insecurity. On the basis of public neighbourhood parks in Villa El Salvador, a city located in the metropolitan region of Lima, Peru, the project identified the technical, social, and municipal components to be considered when deciding which type of food-producing trees to plant and which type of community management to apply. Three factors proved to be essential in integrating food-producing trees in urban forestry: the management of land disputes, the economic potential of productive systems, and the possible conflict between private and public interests. Consultation among all actors in the development of the systems and the coordinating role of the municipality also proved to be important.

Introduction

For many decades, global migration patterns have shifted towards urbanization, leading to the accelerated development of dense, sprawling cities that are increasingly populated. The influx of newcomers and the accompanying intensification of urban activities have substantial negative consequences for the living conditions of the urban population, such as poverty and food insecurity.

Poverty can be defined as a lack of autonomy, security, and power that keeps a person from adequately meeting their needs (Mitlin, 2004). Food insecurity exists when individuals do not have physical or economic access to sufficient, safe, and nutritious food at all times, preventing them from obtaining the energy necessary to lead an active life (FAO, 2009). In the urban context, these two concepts – poverty and food insecurity – are directly related. Since urban families must purchase most of their food and basic services, they are strongly dependent on money (Garrett, 2000; Baker and Schuler, 2004) and are particularly vulnerable to rising food prices (Mitlin, 2004).

To combat this challenge, the poor are increasingly turning to urban agriculture (Binns and Lynch, 1998; Reuther and Dewar, 2005; Levasseur et al., 2007), defined as the action of cultivating plants and raising and keeping animals within the limits of urban zones, either for own consumption or for sale (IPES, 2010). Policy-making has historically drawn a clear distinction between urban agriculture and forestry, the former associated with the fight against food insecurity and the latter with the range of environmental and social services (Figure 1.1). However, merging both functions would allow municipalities to respond, in the same breath, to their social and environmental priorities.

Despite increasing recognition from both scientific and political circles of the effectiveness of urban forestry (see, among others, Nilsson, 2005; Nowak et al., 2006), there is a lack of research and development of implementation strategies (Valaski et al., 2008). In the few studies that refer to the presence of fruit trees in cities, including on private land and in public spaces (Madaleno, 2000; Valaski et al., 2008; Lourdes, 2009), the trees are generally not part of a system specifically set up to exploit the productive potential of green spaces.

This research project aims to determine the interest, viability, and pertinence of the implementation of productive systems based on the plantation

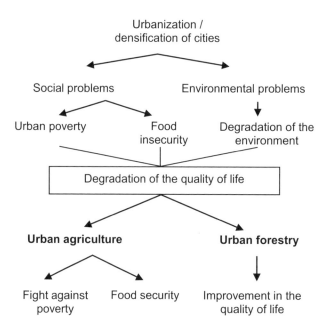

Figure 1.1 Links between agriculture and urban forestry and the main social and environmental problems observed within cities

of food-producing trees in public parks in Villa El Salvador, Peru, with the goal of combating the food insecurity affecting a good part of the population. In doing so, it seeks to develop a precise understanding of the advantages, drawbacks, constraints, and facilitating factors related to the development of productive green spaces within public green spaces, and to quantify the economic impacts of these systems for the households, the community, and the municipality.

Context of the study

Founded in 1971, Villa El Salvador is integrated in the greater metropolitan region of Lima (Figure 1.2). Experiencing major problems of poverty and violence, this municipality of 382,000 inhabitants is witnessing an ongoing exodus of the wealthier citizens to the better neighbourhoods of Lima, leaving the most impoverished people to take their place. As a consequence, the poverty rate in Villa El Salvador is now higher than 72 per cent (Villa El Salvador, 2005).

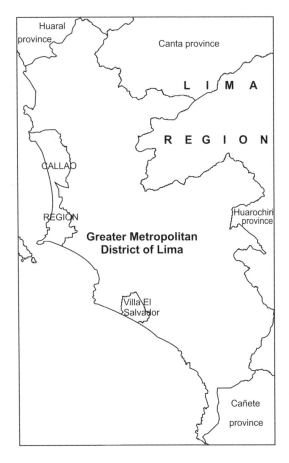

Figure 1.2
Location of Villa El Salvador within the metropolitan region of Lima, Peru

Source:
Based on Carrasco (2005)

The city was formed in the wake of social riots led by the poorest and most marginalized citizens to obtain land rights. As a result, Villa El Salvador is today one of the most active and best-organized cities of greater metropolitan Lima with regard to its social infrastructure. Most of the city's first settlers came from the Andes, where the harsh living conditions of the mountains had given rise to a society geared towards mutual support. In Villa El Salvador, these people then reproduced the structures of mutual help and sharing they were used to in the mountains and organized themselves to ensure that the needs of the entire population were being met. The city today has thousands of social groups involved in all aspects of urban and social development. Among these are neighbourhood watch groups, youth groups, theatre troupes, health collectives, and environmental committees. To assist those who are the most impoverished and to ensure them a basic provision of food, a network of collective kitchens was also set up, the popularity of which also demonstrates the extent of the needs of the population.

Developed according to a carefully crafted urbanization plan, Villa El Salvador is divided into four well demarcated zones: 1) a beach zone; 2) an industrial zone – the economic hub of the municipality; 3) an agricultural zone – designated to ensure food security for the population, but the initial area of which has been reduced by 80 per cent under the pressure of urbanization (Taboada, 2009); and 4) a residential zone. The residential zone is divided into nine sectors, each of which is composed of some 30 residential groups. Each of these residential groups is comprised of 16 neighbourhoods, in turn comprised of 380 private lots each.

A public park spanning roughly 1 ha, at the centre of each residential group, serves as a place of gathering, and contains a sports field, a community centre, and free spaces designated for the planting of trees. However, the majority of these parks have no trees, due to the aridity of the region in which Villa El Salvador is located.

The municipal authorities of Villa El Salvador are nevertheless aware of the wide range of environmental and social benefits related to the presence of trees in the city. A large urban forestry programme was therefore developed with the ambition to create 8 m^2 of green space per inhabitant, which is the amount of space recommended by the World Health Organization (WHO) (Villa El Salvador, 2009). The city's green space development plan adopted in November 2003 lists the technical, administrative, and financial aspects of the management of green spaces, as well as three main objectives: 1) make Villa El Salvador a healthy, clean, and green city that enjoys the active participation of its citizens, young people, and children; 2) develop an integrated environmental management system for green spaces that meets the recreational needs and improves the quality of life of the inhabitants; and 3) contribute to the sustainable development of the municipality (Villa El Salvador, 2006).

This strong political willingness is impeded by a severe lack of human and financial resources, which obliges the municipality to prioritize the greening of some public sectors over others and to rely on citizen involvement to ensure the development of the neighbourhood parks. Most residential groups have, in fact, environmental citizens committees in place, which take charge of the development and maintenance of their respective public parks as well as environmental education programmes.

Conceptual framework of the project

The population of Villa El Salvador is faced with severe poverty problems and a strong dependency on food assistance programmes. At the same time, major efforts are made to increase the municipality's tree coverage. In that context, the inclusion of food-producing trees in the development plans of the neighbourhood parks would respond to both the food and environmental priorities of the municipality and its population.

Objectives and hypotheses

This research project aims to determine the interest, viability, and pertinence of the implementation of productive systems based on the plantation of food-producing trees in neighbourhood parks in order to combat food insecurity. Two main objectives are being pursued: 1) to develop a precise understanding of the advantages, drawbacks, constraints, and facilitating factors related to the development of productive green spaces within public green spaces; and 2) to quantify the economic impacts linked to the implementation of these systems with regard to the households, the community, and the municipality. The development of all research activities is based on three initial hypotheses:

- Hypothesis 1: The integration of food-producing trees within urban public zones, allowing the cultivation of large areas, makes it possible to obtain yields that constitute effective contributions to the fight against food insecurity in the neighbourhoods being studied;
- Hypothesis 2: The possibility of drawing economic benefits and food production from these tree systems significantly promotes the involvement of the community in the maintenance and management of the trees, in turn favouring the longevity of these productive systems and urban forestry projects in general;
- Hypothesis 3: A municipality can draw significant advantages from integrating food-producing trees in its urban forestry plans, whether these are managed by the community or on the basis of a more profit-driven business model.

Theoretical approach

With our project, we aim to encourage the acquisition of practical skills on the basis of an action-research approach. The approach relies on the involvement of the local population, in all development stages of the project, in order to arrive at a better understanding of the situation and to propose pertinent solutions.

Our approach encourages the multi-functional use of public spaces, including the combination of socio-economic, environmental, productive, and other functions in one and the same space (Deelstra et al., 2001; Rodenburg and Nijkamp, 2002).

By definition, a public policy is the reflection of the actions, visions, and orientations defined by a municipality. It guides government action in activity sectors of public interest (Smith, 2003; INRS, 2005; Goffin, 2007). Recognized as occupying a central place in government action (Goffin, 2007), public policy can respond to changes arising in collective life that affect all of society (Smith, 2003). In that context, a public policy can serve to give food-producing trees a set place within urban forestry plans. The required normative framework for such a policy can take shape through a process of reflection undertaken by the municipal government (Goffin, 2007) and by seeking consultation with local actors to ensure that their concerns and priorities are taken into consideration (Smith, 2003).

Research on tree systems has generally been limited to community forestry and social forestry, both systems in which the plantation of trees on public property is based on the participation of the community and the view of reaching purely social objectives (Long and Nair, 1999). With regard to the fight against food insecurity, two complementary approaches are being pursued: ensure the production and supply of a sufficient quality and quantity of products; and improve a population's purchasing power by allowing people to increase their income through the sale of products generated by productive systems (Koc et al., 1999).

Methodology

Diverse data collection and analysis methods were used to determine the interest of the community in the opportunity to ensure food production using the neighbourhood parks and to evaluate economic potential and viability. We proceeded in three stages (Figure 1.3).

Stage 1: Information gathering

In order to gather the information necessary for performing all the analyses, the first stage of the project is comprised of three main components:

- *Technical component.* To ensure the longevity of the implemented systems and to promote the productivity of the trees, the choice of which tree species to use is of crucial importance. The selection should be based on a thorough review of the scientific and technical literature, followed by interviews with the local producers. The trees should be prioritized according to four criteria: 1) need for water, 2) intensity of

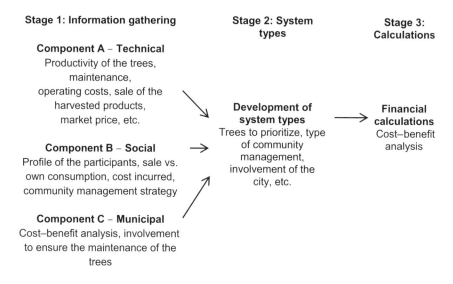

Stage 1: Information gathering

Component A – Technical
Productivity of the trees,
maintenance,
operating costs, sale of the
harvested products,
market price, etc.

Component B – Social
Profile of the participants, sale vs.
own consumption, cost incurred,
community management strategy

Component C – Municipal
Cost–benefit analysis, involvement
to ensure the maintenance of the
trees

Stage 2: System types

Development of system types
Trees to prioritize, type
of community
management,
involvement of the
city, etc.

Stage 3: Calculations

Financial calculations
Cost–benefit
analysis

Figure 1.3 Illustration of the main stages of the research project

management to ensure a good yield, 3) resistance to pests, and 4) resistance to salinity.

- *Social component.* As the project is based on citizen involvement, the participation of the communities affected by the redevelopment of their neighbourhood park is essential. Discussion panels were thus organized with four environmental committees to understand their vision of the development of the parks and to identify the main facilitating and inhibiting factors likely to influence the implementation of the developed productive strategy. To that effect, we organized participatory workshops that made use of maps and schematic diagrams, a SWOT (strengths, weaknesses, opportunities, and threats) analysis, and a semi-directed group discussion.

Following the discussion panels, semi-directed interviews were realized with each participant to allow them to consolidate their understanding and to identify which factors they considered to be a priority for the project. The questionnaires were developed according to the stated-choice method, following the recommendations of Louviere et al. (2000), Boxall and Beckley (2002), Holmes and Adamowicz (2003), and Powe (2007).

- *Municipal component.* Semi-directed interviews were also conducted with political representatives of Villa El Salvador to discuss the advantages and drawbacks related to the introduction of food-producing trees within the municipal public parks and of incorporating such systems into the urban forestry policy. The topic of maintenance and management tasks that could be delegated to the municipality was also discussed.

Stages 2 and 3: System types and financial calculations

Using all the information gathered during the first stage, development plans for the parks under study were proposed and then approved by the heads of the environmental committees. This then served as a basis for the financial calculations. The profitability, pertinence, and feasibility of the implementation of food-producing tree systems in the neighbourhood parks were then evaluated according to three financial criteria:

1   The net present value (NPV), obtained by subtracting the total costs (C) from the total benefits (B), in using present values (Scott and Betters, 2000; Veeman and Luckert, 2002).
2   The cost–benefit ratio (CBR), which allows establishment of the effectiveness of the allocation of resources (Tesileanu, 2008). It consists of the division of the total benefits by the total costs, using the present values (Veeman and Luckert, 2002).
3   The internal rate of return (IRR), which expresses 'the potential for having benefits above costs as a percentage' (Veeman and Luckert, 2002: 15) and consists of determining the compound interest rate, the benefits of which are equal to the costs, in present value.

Three analysis levels were taken into account: the household, the community, and the municipality. The total costs incurred by performing productive activities include, among others, input costs, labour costs, opportunity costs for land usage, and transportation and marketing costs. The benefits considered, for their part, represent all the direct and indirect revenues obtained from the productive activities, such as the sale of the products and the value of the portion consumed by the producers themselves.

This research methodology, based mainly on the discussions and consultations with the local population and the municipal authorities, can be easily adapted to many countries and municipalities and to very different contexts. It was developed to promote a true social and institutional infrastructure, an essential condition for the replicability of the project. However, in the case of municipalities that do not have a social structure that is as supportive as that of Villa El Salvador, the application of the method would require an additional initial stage comprised of community organization and discussion panels with local actors interested in participating in an analysis of the environmental, social, and economic characteristics of their community.

Analysis

The scarcity of vacant spaces as a result of urban development calls for innovative strategies to ensure the optimal use of land, while also maintaining the multi-functional use of spaces. One such strategy is the introduction of productive components within the development plans of recreational public spaces. However, the development of such productive strategies is subjected to a variety of facilitating and inhibiting factors.

The absence of land disputes

The development of a city is characterized by an ongoing conflict (Torre et al., 2006) consisting of a continuous series of disputes over the competing uses of spaces. The outcome of these disputes depends, among other factors, on the size of the area in question, the land market regulations, and the zoning regulations established by the municipality (Villeneuve and Côté, 1994).

Over the course of the development and densification of a built framework, the increasing scarcity of vacant spaces raises the value of land according to market regulations, thereby increasing the opportunity cost linked to each usage of the land. In such a context, the conservation of land for activities that do not generate high profits, such as urban agriculture, is not met with much interest. As a result, urban producers often have no choice but to set up their cultivations on land lent to them on a temporary basis only. In this way, they find themselves in a permanent state of land insecurity, which is considered one of the most limiting factors for the development of food production in the city (Reuther and Dewar, 2005).

In the meantime, the conservation of green spaces and urban public parks is becoming a development priority thanks to the growing recognition of the environmental and social benefits offered by trees. These relatively large spaces are protected from land development by different municipal zoning laws, constituting a tenure security that is essential for the long-term exploitation of land. This advantage is also fundamental to planning a plantation of food-producing trees, which, reaching its full productive potential only within several decades, requires a long-term vision.

An economic potential not to be overestimated

Even if the use of productive systems based on the plantation of food-producing trees allows large-scale areas to be put into production and to obtain interesting yields, the real economic potential of such a project should be carefully analysed to avoid overestimation.

The economic profitability of the implemented tree systems is strongly influenced by the objectives of the community in charge of the systems' management, the number of actors directly involved in the maintenance, the harvests, as well as the quality of the maintenance. These factors, which are the same factors to which food security programmes for households or entire communities are subjected, should thus be taken into account in the development of projects.

Opposition between individual and collective appropriation

The interest demonstrated by citizens in the maintenance of productive systems is usually directly linked to their prospect of being remunerated for their efforts with food products. In that sense, public spaces are being appropriated for private means, which constitutes a conflict of interest and threatens to limit the acceptance of the project by the community as a whole. For example, mango, papaya, apple, and fig trees, along with other fruit trees from productive systems produce popular and tasty foods that are easily accessible to all visitors of a park. When walking through the park, these people may well feel entitled to appropriate what they find in that public space, rather than acknowledging that that privilege is reserved for those involved in maintaining the trees. The community thus has to anticipate theft problems, which, in turn, risk generating a strongly conflictual context within the parks, leading to a significant degradation of the relations between producers and visitors. Given that a public space should, by definition, remain accessible to the entire community, this problem calls for the development of strategies other than the simple restriction of physical access to the park.

One such strategy could be to create fences protecting those trees that are most vulnerable to theft. Moreover, park guardians could be hired and paid from the income generated from the sale of the harvests. Another option could be to prioritize trees that produce fruit which has to be processed in order to be edible, which makes them less attractive to visitors.

Over the long term, any solution would need to incorporate an awareness-raising component so that the entire community could learn to recognize the social and environmental importance of the project. In this way, the users of the park would identify with and engage voluntarily in the protection of the food-producing tree systems. Such a campaign would have to be geared specifically to the environment in question (Photo 1.1) and emphasize the importance of good communication between the diverse users of the park.

The objective of the productive systems could also be revised so as to facilitate the acceptance by all. This could, for example, include the goal of improving food security for the entire community by interlinking the project with a local food-support programme such as collective kitchens. The expected effect of such a sharing of the harvests is based on the premise that, aware of the importance of these harvests for the community benefit, many users would eventually identify with the park in different ways and, as stewards of the productive systems so to speak, promote the longevity of the project.

Consultation throughout the planning: Choosing the right neighbourhood policy

The overall success of a food-producing tree project relies on the good communication between the diverse actors involved, as well as a thorough analysis of the strategies that allow the preservation of harmony among the users of the

Mariève Lafontaine-Messier

Photo 1.1
Awareness-raising strategy
implemented by the citizens
of Villa El Salvador

park. Citizens must also be given the means to develop an emotional attachment to the productive systems, thereby empowering them with a sense of agency with regard to the project (Moser, 2009).

This condition is ideally provided for at a broader level in the form of a neighbourhood policy. In reference to 'the choice by means of which the [neighbourhood] evolves based on a notion of [neighbourhood] that is specific to itself' (Rossi, 2001: 112), such a policy would be based on the mobilization of the population around a common development objective. As a vector of the identity of a community, the policy takes shape by matching and reconciling the perceived environment and the goals and sensibilities of each participant (Moser, 2009).

A park, being the heart of a neighbourhood and allowing for the gathering of a community, is a space in which citizens form opinions (Zepf, 2004). In that sense, a food-production project within a public park should be consistent with the neighbourhood policy defined by each community through its everyday activities. For example, the objective aimed for by the production, whether this be commercialization, own consumption, or food assistance for residents, should clearly reflect the community spirit of the residents and play on the image projected by the latter. For this reason, the interests, vision, and priorities of each resident should be discussed and taken into account in the realization of projects.

The centralizing role of the municipality

While the daily management of productive systems relies on the involvement of the local community, the municipality also plays an important role at many levels. First, a public park is subject to municipal governance, explaining the necessity to obtain its consent prior to setting up productive systems. Moreover, despite the fact that a municipality only stands to gain from local initiatives in urban forestry, the use of public land should be governed by official agreements between the users and the municipality, clearly defining the roles and responsibilities of each.

Further, a centralized supervision of the maintenance of the trees, in particular with regard to monitoring the appearance of diseases and pests, is crucial for ensuring the adequate protection of the entire municipal tree cover. The diverse body of citizen actors not specialized in the field of productive trees, yet involved in the management of a multitude of systems implemented in many residential groups, leads to a great heterogeneity of actions. As a result, certain zones become possibly more prone to negligence than others. However, a forest canopy of a city is ultimately one contiguous system in which all trees are interrelated. For that reason, the outbreak of a disease within the tree system of one residential group can spread rapidly and lead to major damages of all food-producing trees in the city, explaining the importance of standardizing the monitoring process and of centralizing it at the municipal scale.

The municipality should allocate the necessary resources for hiring specialists in urban forestry and in the management of food-producing trees, which could well represent a major financial challenge. However, such an investment is justifiable given the scope of the environmental and social services offered by the development and maintenance of a tree cover that is dense and in good health.

The role of public policies

In Villa El Salvador, the population's desire for an improvement of the nutritional quality of their food supply and the expansion of the municipal forest cover are taken into account within the Comprehensive Development Plan of Villa El Salvador devised for the year 2021 (Villa El Salvador, 2006). The importance of food production in the urban milieu is lobbied for by a set of local actors who are promoting this issue before the political authorities. Moreover, the municipality has clearly stated that it views urban forestry and the development of green spaces as a high priority. The fact that the plantation of food-producing trees allows the pursuit of two goals at the same time, namely, the expansion of the forest cover and food security, makes it a welcome proposal.

It is thus up to the public authorities to go through with the project and to incorporate these priorities in a clear and prescriptive plan that defines the roles and responsibilities of the actors and that seeks a consensus between the sometimes divergent interests of those actors (Goffin, 2007). As the productive strategy described here relies in great part on citizen involvement, and given the multiplicity of the actors concerned, the final policy should be the result of a process of consultation and cooperation (Smith, 2003). This process is all the more important as the implementation of a public policy is directly linked to the degree to which the actors responsible for the realization of the objectives eventually come to identify with the project (Goffin, 2007).

Conclusions

This action-research project evaluated the feasibility of the creation of productive systems based on the implementation of food-producing trees within public neighbourhood parks in Villa El Salvador, Peru. Under community management, and allowing for food production in the urban setting, these systems have an interesting potential to contribute to the fight against food insecurity, while allowing residents to benefit from the environmental services provided by trees. Moreover, the use of public spaces circumvents the critical challenge of land disputes between real estate development and urban agriculture, while guaranteeing the longevity of the productive systems.

However, several factors that may complicate the implementation of these systems must be taken into consideration. First, any action undertaken within a space designated for public use should be planned in consultation with the diverse actors affected by the project and undertaken in agreement with a neighbourhood policy developed by the local community. Given that these systems produce edible and marketable products, they blur the boundaries between the public and the private sphere, potentially making them less welcomed by some users of the park. Despite a certain market potential, the economic interests linked to the sale of the harvested products depend on a variety of factors and should not be overestimated. Lastly, the large-scale development of a productive strategy of this type requires the active participation of the municipality, which is owner of the land and the only body capable of coordinating all management efforts.

Certain in-depth analyses still need to be conducted to determine the actual potential of food-producing trees to provide food security. First, the productive performance of food-producing trees implemented in the urban setting and under community management should be evaluated to anticipate potential drops in yield. At the social level, the interactions between the various actors affected by the productive systems implemented are also worthy of further research to identify the main causes of conflict between the members of the community. The modes of organization of the producers, the actual impact on the food security of the local community, and the value of introducing units for processing the products are other pertinent subjects that merit further examination.

These productive systems are transferable to a larger scale. In greater metropolitan Lima, many municipalities have environmental and socio-economic characteristics similar to those of Villa El Salvador. If implemented in all municipalities of the region, productive systems based on the plantation of food-producing trees in public parks could, in the long term, constitute a green belt around the Peruvian capital. This innovative project is also applicable on a global level. The urban sprawl of the majority of big cities in the world is due mainly to the expansion of areas occupied by marginal neighbourhoods characterized by high degrees of poverty and food insecurity.

References

Baker, J. and Schuler, N. (2004) 'Analyzing urban poverty: A summary of methods and approaches', World Bank Policy Research Working Paper No. 3399, World Bank, Washington DC, http://ssrn.com/abstract=625276 [accessed 14 November 2009].

Bellefontaine, R., Petit, S., Orcet, M. P., Deleporte, P., and Bertault, J.-G. (2001) *Les arbres hors forêts, Vers une meilleure prise en compte*, Food and Agriculture Organization of the United Nations, Rome, www.fao.org/docrep/005/Y2328F/y2328f00.htm [accessed 25 March 2009].

Binns, T. and Lynch, K. (1998) 'Feeding Africa's growing cities into the 21st century: The potential of urban agriculture', *Journal of International Development* 10(6): 777–93.

Boxall, P. C. and Beckley, T. (2002) 'An introduction to approaches and issues for measuring non-market values in developing economies', in B. M. Campbell and M. K. Luckert (eds) *Uncovering the Hidden Harvest – Valuation Methods for Woodland and Forest Resources*, pp. 103–40, Earthscan, London.

Carrasco, T. (2005) 'Map of metropolitan Lima', http://commons.wikimedia.org/wiki/File:Map_of_Metropolitan_Lima.PNG [accessed 3 August 2011].

Deelstra, T., Boyd, D., and van den Biggelaar, M. (2001). 'Multifunctional land use: An opportunity for promoting urban agriculture in Europe', *Urban Agriculture Magazine* 4: 33–5.

FAO (Food and Agriculture Organization of the United Nations) (2009) *Déclaration du Sommet mondial sur la sécurité alimentaire*, World Food Summit, 16–18 November, Rome, www.fao.org/WFS/index_fr.htm [accessed 1 February 2010].

Garrett, J. (2000) 'Achieving urban food and nutrition security in the developing world, an overview', Focus 3, Brief 1, International Food Policy Research Institute, Washington DC.

Goffin, C. (2007) 'Les politiques publiques', Université de Pau et des Pays de l'Adour, UFR pluridisciplinaire de Bayonne, Projet Interform, Seminar from 3–4 April, Pau, France.

Holmes, T. P. and Adamovicz, W. L. (2003) 'Attribute-based methods', in P. A. Champ, K. J. Boyle, and T. C. Brown (eds) *The Economics of Non-Market Goods and Resources: A Primer on Nonmarket Valuation*, pp. 171–220, Kluwer Academic Publishers, Norwell.

INRS (Institut National de Recherche Scientifique) (2005) 'Qu'est-ce qu'une politique publique?', Institut National de Recherche Scientifique, Quebec, http://partenariat-familles.inrs-ucs.uquebec.ca/DocsPDF/fiche2.pdf [accessed 5 July 2010].

IPES (2010) 'Définicion de la agricultura urbana', IPES Agricultura Urbana, www.ipes.org/index.php?option=com_content&view=article&id=92&Itemid=11 [accessed 6 February 2010].

Koc, M., MacRae, R., Mougeot, L. J. A., and Weish, J. (1999) *For Hunger-Proof Cities: Sustainable Urban Food Systems*, International Development Research Centre, Ottawa.

Konijnendijk, C. C., Robert, M. R., Kenney, A., and Randrup, T. B. (2006) 'Defining urban forestry – A comparative perspective of North America and Europe', *Urban Forestry & Urban Greening* 4: 93–103.

Levasseur, V, Pasquini, M. W., Kouamé, C., and Temple, L. (2007) 'A review of urban and peri-urban vegetable production in West Africa', *Acta Horticulturae* 762: 245–52.

Long, A. J. and Nair, P. K. R. (1999) 'Trees outside forests: Agro-, community, and urban forestry', *New Forests* 17: 145–74.

Lourdes, S. O. (2009) 'Evaluación de los árboles fuera del bosque en el consejo popular Pogoloti – Finlay – Belen – Husillo, para el beneficio del programa nacional de agricultura urbana', thesis, Titulo de Master en Agricultura Urbana, Instituto de Investigaciones Fundamentales de Agricultura Tropical Alejandro de Humboldt, Havana.

Louviere, J. J., Hensher, D. A., and Swait, J. D. (2000) *Stated-Choice Methods: Analysis and Applications*, Cambridge University Press, Cambridge.

Madaleno, I. (2000) 'Urban agriculture in Belém, Brazil', *Cities* 17(1): 73–7.

Mitlin, D. (2004) 'Understanding urban poverty: What the poverty reduction strategy papers tell us', *Human Settlements Working Paper Series Poverty Reduction in Urban Areas No. 13*, International Institute for Environment and Development, London.

Moser, G. (2009) *Psychologie environnementale – Les relations homme-environnement*, Éditions De Boeck Université, Brussels.

Nilsson, K. (2005) 'Urban forestry as a vehicle for healthy and sustainable development', *Chinese Forestry Science and Technology* 4(1): 1–14.

Nowak, D. J., Crane, D. E., and Stevens, J. C. (2006) 'Air pollution removal by urban trees and shrubs in the United States', *Urban Forestry & Urban Greening* 4: 115–23.

Powe, N. A. (2007) *Redesigning Environmental Valuation – Mixing Methods Within Stated Preference Techniques*, Edward Elgar, Cheltenham.

Reuther, S. and Dewar, N. (2005) 'Competition for the use of public open space in low-income urban areas: The economic potential of urban gardening in Khayelitsha, Cape Town', *Development Southern Africa/Development Bank of Southern Africa* 23(1): 97–122.

Rodenburg, C. A. and Nijkamp, P. (2002) 'Multifunctional land use in the city: Research memorandum 2002-25', *Built Environment – Special Issue: Multifunctional Urban Land Use as a New Planning Challenge*, Faculty of Economics and Business Administration, Department of Spatial Economics, Free University, Amsterdam.

Rossi, A. (2001) *L'architecture de la ville*, InFolio éditions, Gollion, Switzerland.

Scott, J. L. and Betters, D. R. (2000) 'Economic analysis of urban tree replacement decisions', *Journal of Arboriculture* 26(2): 69–77.

Smith, B. L. (2003) *Public Policy and Public Participation Engaging Citizens and Community in the Development of Public Policy*, Population and Public

Health Branch Atlantic Regional Office Health Canada, Halifax.

Taboada, S. (2009) *Informe sobre el contexto local de Villa El Salvador, primera version*, IPES – Promocion del Desarrollo Sostenible, Lima.

Tesileanu, R. (2008) 'Valuing non-market environmental goods: A critical analysis of various valuation methods', Diploma Thesis, Institute of Forest Economics, University of Freiburg, Freiburg, Germany.

Torre, A., Aznar, O., Bonin, M., Caron, A., Chia, E., Galman, M., Lefranc, Ch., Melot, R., Guérin, M., Jeanneaux, Ph., Kirat, Th., Paoli, J. C., Salazar, M. I., and Thinon, P. (2006) 'Conflits et tensions autour des usages de l'espace dans les territoires ruraux et périurbains – Le cas de six zones géographiques françaises', *Revue d'Économie Régionale & Urbaine* 2006(3): 415–553.

Valaski, S., Adenilson de Carvalho, J., and Nucci, J. C. (2008) 'Arvores frutiferas na arborizacao de calcadas do bairro Santa Felicidade – Curitiba/Pr e seus beneficios para a sociedade', *Geografia. Ensino & Pesquisa* 12: 972–85.

Veeman, T. S. and Luckert, M. K. (2002) 'Economic decision-making frameworks for considering resource values: Procedures, perils and promise', in B. M. Campbell and M. K. Luckert (eds) *Uncovering the Hidden Harvest – Valuation Methods for Woodland and Forest Resources,* pp. 141–67, Earthscan, London.

Villa El Salvador (2005) 'Diagnostico de Villa El Salvador – Aspecto economico', www.munives.gob.pe/Ves_Diagnostico.htm [accessed 13 October 2009].

Villa El Salvador (2006) *Plan intégral de développement concerté: Villa El Salvador à l'horizon 2021 – Résumé*, Municipalité de Villa El Salvador, www.munives. gob.pe/PlanIntegral/Resumen Ampliado.pdf [accessed 25 April 2009].

Villa El Salvador (2009) *Portal municipal de Villa El Salvador*, www.munives. gob.pe/Mun_PidMunives.htm [accessed 26 April 2009].

Villeneuve, P. and Côté, G. (1994) 'Conflits de localisation et étalement urbain: y a-t-il un lien?', *Cahiers de Géographie du Québec* 38(105): 397–412.

Zepf, M. (2004) 'Action publique, métropolisation et espaces publics – Les enjeux du débat', in Zepf, M. (ed.) *Concerter, gouverner et concevoir les espaces publics urbains*, pp. 1–14, Presses polytechniques et universitaires romandes, Lausanne, Switzerland.

About the author

Mariève Lafontaine-Messier lives and works in Peru for Desarrollo Rural Sustentable (DRIS), a Peruvian NGO focusing on rural development and the conservation of natural resources. She holds a bachelor's degree in agronomy and a master's degree in integrated rural development from Université Laval, Canada, and is currently completing a master's degree in agroforestry, also at Université Laval. She has worked as a project manager for the urban agriculture and forestry programme of Vrac Environnement, an environmental NGO based in Montreal, Canada, and has interned with the United Nations Urban Forestry programme, where she worked on the advancement of urban forestry around the world.

Chapter 2

Urban agriculture in Dakar, Senegal: Health aspects related to polluted irrigation water

Mamadou Lamine Ndiaye

Abstract

The aim of this action-research project was to identify the effects of polluted irrigation water used in urban agriculture in Dakar, Senegal, on human health, in particular the health of children. The project comprised a comparative epidemiological study between exposed and non-exposed populations. The results showed that in the exposed populations, the prevalence of diarrhoea in children between 0 and 15 years of age was 46 per cent, whereas in the non-exposed population, the prevalence of diarrhoea was 16 per cent. A logistic regression model indicated that the children from the exposed sites had a 21-fold greater risk of contracting diarrhoea than did the children from the non-exposed site. The most important risk factor seemed to be the consumption of local groundwater (water from manual wells or from manual pumps). The study shows that irrigation with polluted water has impacts on human health and makes important recommendations for minimizing the risks.

Introduction

Faced with galloping population growth, cities in the Global South are experiencing food insecurity and high levels of unemployment. Urban agriculture, an activity in full throttle, seems to be an interesting alternative for providing cities with fresh vegetables. In the region of Dakar, Senegal, 70 per cent of the supply of vegetables comes from urban agriculture (Mbaye, 1999), and similar trends have been reported in other countries in the Global South, such as Ghana and Mali (Smith, 2002). However, this expansion is slowing down due to problems of water shortages and excessive land use. Presently, 70 per cent of the world's fresh water is used for agricultural purposes, and in the Global South, that proportion is above 95 per cent (UN-Water, 2006). The overexploitation of groundwater bodies lowers the water table and contributes to a deterioration of water quality (through salinization), which in turn leads to the increased use of raw wastewater and organic manure for agriculture. These types of practices are not without consequences for the environment and the health of populations. The use of raw wastewater for irrigation and the spreading of organic manure on soil are often blamed for the microbiological and chemical contamination of groundwater (Ensink et al., 2002; Hussain et al., 2002; Van der Hoek et al., 2002; Majdoub et al., 2003; Bolster et al., 2006) and agricultural products (Rosas et al., 1984; Al-Lahham et al., 2003; Amoah et al., 2005; Ibenyassine et al., 2006) as well as for public health problems.

The consumption of non-potable water is among the major causes of mortality and morbidity in the world (OECD, 2003). For example, approximately 88 per cent of diarrhoea cases in the world are attributed to the consumption of non-potable water, inadequate sanitation, and insufficient hygiene, and account for 1.5 million deaths each year, many of which are among children (Prüss-Üstün et al., 2008). The frequency of food-borne diseases caused by pathogenic bacteria continues to increase at an alarming rate in the Global North and Global South alike (Lampel et al., 2000). According to Mensah (2005), 30,660 children die each year due to the consumption of contaminated food.

Studies conducted in Burkina Faso, Morocco (Melloul and Hassani, 1999), Pakistan, and Vietnam (Trang et al., 2007) have demonstrated the impact of the use of polluted water in urban agriculture on the health of riparian populations. However, few studies exist on the impact of this issue in Senegal. Our study aims to address this gap in the knowledge of the health impacts of polluted irrigation water used in the urban agriculture of Dakar.

Context of the study

The region of Dakar is experiencing dramatic demographic growth, as are most city regions of the Global South. The growth rate of the urban population rose from 21 per cent to 53 per cent between 1955 and 1999 (DPS, 2003). Spread over a surface of 550 km² (0.28 per cent of the territory of Senegal), Dakar is home to a fifth of the national population, representing a density of over 4,000 habitants per km² (ANSD, 2007).

To ensure food safety, urban agriculture has been extensively developed over the past 10 years in a region with favourable hydrological and climatic conditions: the Niayes region. However, the Niayes ecosystem is very fragile as its very shallow groundwater body is vulnerable to salt-water intrusion. The heavy reliance on this precious resource to serve agricultural purposes has provoked groundwater depletion and has accelerated the salinization process, i.e. the rate of salt-water intrusion. This has prompted farmers to use a lot of organic manure and raw wastewater to improve yields. Furthermore, the health status of the population of the Dakar region is extremely poor, showing a prevalence of cholera, typhoid, and paratyphoid epidemics, as well as very frequent episodes of diarrhoea.

The origin of these epidemics has been questioned. According to Gaye and Niang (2002), the outbreak of epidemics in Senegal over the past 10 years could be attributable to the polluted water from urban agriculture. However, while the impact of wastewater on the health of farmers is well documented (Niang, 2002; Faruqui et al., 2004; Baldé, 2005), research on the local populations is not exhaustive.

Hypotheses of our study

Our working hypotheses are succinctly illustrated in Figure 2.1. Namely, the use of raw wastewater for irrigation and the abusive use of organic manure for soil amendment in urban agriculture can lead to the microbiological contamination of the groundwater and the vegetables produced. As a result, the local populations consuming either the vegetables or the water contaminated by the wells or manual pumps get sick.

Materials and methods

Analysis of the health data obtained from the health districts Dominique (Pikine) and Nabil Choucker (Patte d'Oie) showed that during the first half of 2008, diarrhoeal disease was the second and third highest cause of morbidity among the populations of Pikine and Patte d'Oie respectively (Figures 2.2 and 2.3) and affected children the most. For this reason, a main focus of our study was the children living in proximity to the agricultural sites in Pikine and Patte d'Oie. This population was compared with that of Dène, located in the Rufisque department (control site) at a distance of about 40 km from Dakar. Dène exhibits the same socio-economic characteristics as Pikine and Patte

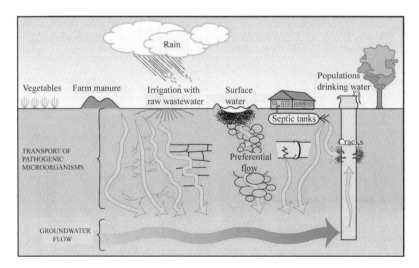

Figure 2.1 Illustration of the research hypotheses

Source: Modified from Majdoub et al. (2003)

d'Oie; however the fields are irrigated exclusively with groundwater (water from shallow, hand-dug wells called *céanes*). The characteristics of the sites of study are summarized in Table 2.1.

Sampling

The local populations of Pikine and Patte d'Oie were considered as the *exposed population* and that of Dène as the *non-exposed population,* i.e. exposed or non-exposed to the usage of polluted water for the irrigation of fields. For the purposes of our study, our definition of diarrhoea was

Table 2.1 Characteristics of the study sites

Characteristics	Study sites		
	Pikine	Patte d'Oie	Dène
Irrigated area (ha)	49.9	12	
Production of lettuce (tonne/year)	3,544	560	
Type of irrigation water	*Céanes,* wastewater	*Céanes,* wells, wastewater	*Céanes,* wells
Number of farmers	830	161	
Population[1]	161,438	29,812	

Source: Data for [1] from ANSD (2007)

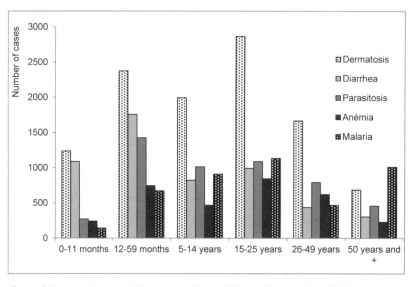

Figure 2.2 Health data of the population of Pikine (first half of 2008)

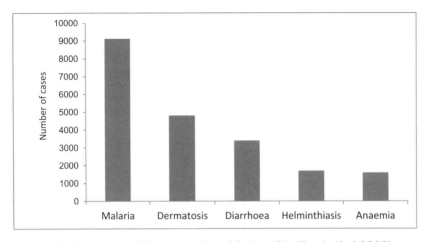

Figure 2.3 Health data of the population of Patte d'Oie (first half of 2008)

that of the surveyed populations, mainly because many studies have shown that the reliability of surveys on diarrhoea could be higher if they were based on the definition of diarrhoea used by the subjects themselves and not that of WHO (Gagneux et al., 1999). Three trained survey takers visited the sites, and the households surveyed were randomly selected. The size of the sample was estimated starting from the size of the population and by referring to the estimation table of Mayer and Ouellet (1991) for a confidence level of 95 per cent and a precision of ± 5 per cent. The surveys were conducted between the months of July and October 2008. The questionnaire included 147 variables concerning the consumption of groundwater, vegetables, the prevalence of diarrhoea, and risk factors. A total of 1,165 surveys were conducted.

Analysis of the data

The data of the comparative study were captured with SPSS Data Entry 4.0. A multiple correspondence analysis (MCA) with Statistica 8.0 then allowed for the selection of variables that were meaningful with regard to the occurrence of diarrhoea in children. These variables were then included in a multivariate analysis by applying the logistic regression model using SPSS 16.0.

Results

Characteristics of the studied sites

Pikine site stands out for its dwelling types (shacks or dwellings made of adobe) that reflect the poverty in this zone. The humidity that prevails in these types of housing promotes the proliferation of flies and cockroaches.

Moreover, the majority of households (90 per cent) use water from manual pumps (groundwater) for drinking and cooking water. This is due to their lack of means to pay for running water or, for those who do have running water, its displeasing reddish colour or nauseating odour.

The Patte d'Oie site is characterized by a high level of education of the population (secondary level to university), by the population's practice of disinfecting lettuce with chlorine before consumption, as well as the use of groundwater (manual water pumps, well water).

Dène is distinguished for the systematic use of well water for drinking and cooking (100 per cent of the households), a high number of children, and a low level of education (primary level).

Prevalence of diarrhoea

The analysis is based on 1,165 questionnaires. The results of the study showed that the prevalence of diarrhoea in children of the exposed population was 46 per cent, while it was 16 per cent ($\chi^2 = 97.3$, $p = 0.0001$) for the non-exposed population. The percentages of the most recent episodes of diarrhoea preceding the interviews among the exposed populations are listed in Table 2.2.

Risk factors of diarrhoea

The MCA allowed us to determine the variables that seem to be related to the outbreak of diarrhoea in children. In the regression model developed in this study (1), the risk factors for the occurrence of diarrhoea (ψ) were studied in relation with the hygiene of the children (β) and the home (α), the level of education of the parents (γ), the degree of privacy in the living quarters for each family member (δ), the consumption of lettuce by the children (χ), the treatment of the lettuce prior to consumption (ε), the drinking water (φ), the cooking water (ρ), and the site (σ). For the analysis, the lowest level (0) was considered as the base level. The confidence interval (CI) was 95 per cent and a variable is considered as meaningful if $p < 0.05$.

Table 2.2 Percentage of the populations under study in 2008 suffering from an episode of diarrhoea preceding the surveys

	Last episode			
Population	One day ago (%)	One week ago (%)	One month ago (%)	More than one month ago (%)
Exposed (n = 774 [§])	10	19	25	42
Non-exposed (n = 391)	0.2	2	5	10

Note: [§]n = number of respondents

$$\Psi\,(0,1) = \beta\,(0,1)^*\alpha\,(0,1)^*\gamma\,(0,1)^*\delta\,(0,1)^*\chi\,(0,1)^*\varepsilon\,(0,1)^*\varphi$$
$$(0,1,2)^*\rho\,(0,1,2)^*\sigma\,(0,1)^*\Omega^*\Phi \tag{1}$$

Ω: Interaction between the variables α, δ, γ

Φ: Interaction between the variables σ, χ, ε

The results showed that the children living in the exposed sites (Pikine and Patte d'Oie) are 21 times more at risk of getting diarrhoea than those of the control site (Dène) (OR (odds ratio) = 21.1, p = 0.0001). The children who drank groundwater ($\varphi 1$) from the exposed sites had a 3.8-fold higher risk of getting diarrhoea than those from the non-exposed site (OR = 3.8, p = 0.007). The hygiene in the household (α) (OR = 0.37, p = 0.0001) and the hygiene of the children (β) (OR = 0.43, p = 0.0001) had protective effects, as did the disinfection of lettuce (ε) prior to consumption (OR = 0.34, p = 0.0001). The consumption of lettuce by the children (χ) appears to have a protective effect (OR = 0.33, p = 0.005).

A gender-specific analysis

The epidemiological investigation showed that women are responsible for the households. Indeed, for the exposed populations, 80 per cent of the people available for an interview were women; for the control population, this percentage was 83 per cent. This tendency can be explained by the traditional values and customs under which women are primarily those in charge of the household. However, women also play a vital role in the retail of the vegetables produced by the urban agriculture of Dakar, especially in the case of lettuce. In the farms, women represent potential buyers, and in the markets, they do 100 per cent of the selling. Thus, women's role in the process of non-contamination of lettuce is crucial (Ndiaye, 2009).

Discussion

The epidemiological results (comparative study) seem to indicate a cause–effect relationship between urban agriculture and the health of the local populations of the agricultural sites. The greatest risk factor for the occurrence of diarrhoea in children appears to be the consumption of groundwater around the urban agriculture sites (OR = 3.8, CI: 1.4–10). A study of the impact of polluted water used in urban agriculture on the groundwater showed that the microbiological quality of water from supply points around the sites was indeed lower, especially during the rainy season (Ndiaye, 2009). Faecal coliform organisms were detected in the water from wells and manual pumps, in particular around the Pikine site. Drinking water should be exempt of faecal coliform organisms (WHO, 2006). Diarrhoeal diseases are generally caused by the ingestion of pathogenic organisms contained either in water, on dirty food, or on dirty hands (Prüss-Üstün et al., 2008). A study conducted in Mauritania with the urban farmers of Nouakchott showed that the use of non-protected well water was responsible for 59.2 per cent of the cases of diarrhoea among the farmers of Tel Zatar (Gagneux et al., 1999). Also, a recent study in Hanoi (Vietnam) showed that the incidences of diarrhoea among farmers and aquaculturists using wastewater was due to the consumption of well water, raw vegetables, and the failure to wash hands after defecation (Trang et al., 2007).

The consumption of lettuce does not seem to have an impact on the prevalence of diarrhoea in children (OR = 0.3, CI: 0.1–0.7). A study on the impact of polluted water and the mode of treatment of lettuce revealed elevated concentrations of *E. coli*, above the standards of the International Commission for Microbiological Specifications for Foods (ICMSF, 1986), as well as *Salmonella* sp. contamination (Ndiaye, 2009). This result can be explained by the interrelation between the site, the children's consumption of lettuce, and the treatment of lettuce prior to consumption (Φ) (OR = 3.5, CI: 1.4–8.9). The Patte d'Oie site had more children who consumed lettuce (20 per cent) compared with the Pikine site (8 per cent). Moreover, 86 per cent of the families in Patte d'Oie reported that they disinfect lettuce with Javel water before consumption, compared with 46 per cent in Pikine. Also, according to Beuchat (1998), the simple practice of vigorously cleaning fruits and vegetables with drinking water reduces the microbial load by 10 to 100 times. However, of the total number of children suffering from diarrhoea in the exposed sites, 30 per cent consumed lettuce. Of those, 21 per cent came from Patte d'Oie and 9 per cent from Pikine. In the control population, this dropped to 4 per cent.

Given that urban agriculture is an integral part of daily life in the region of Dakar due to its economic and social importance, local authorities would do well to regulate this sector on the basis of these scientific data. The use of raw wastewater for agriculture is prohibited by international institutions such as WHO and Senegal's national institutions, such as through the Code d'hygiène (Assemblée Nationale, 1983). The results of this work could thus serve the government, researchers, and NGOs with a starting point for finding sustainable solutions to minimize health impacts. During our results workshop at the Institut Fondamental d'Afrique Noire (IFAN) of the Université de Dakar, the director of the NGO ENDA-RUP highly appreciated and valued our research topic, as it was of major relevance to a project on the quality of vegetables in Dakar which his organization was conducting in partnership with WHO. The daily journal *Le Soleil* published on 29 January 2010: 'The City of Dakar and FAO yesterday announced, at City Hall, the launch of the project *Promotion of the use of quality water for urban and peri-urban agriculture*, an economic, social, financial, and environmental project with a budget of US$1,053,293 (more than 526 million CFA francs) of the Spanish Cooperation to Combat Clandestine Migration'.

Conclusions

The prevalence of diarrhoea in children of the exposed population seems to indicate that urban agriculture could have negative health impacts on populations. The microbiological contamination of the groundwater through agricultural activities seems to be the main problem. Indeed, the consumption of water from wells and manual pumps situated near the Pikine and Patte d'Oie sites was assumed to be the greatest risk factor for the occurrence of diarrhoea in children. Despite the contamination level of lettuce (very high density of *E. coli* and detection of *Salmonella* sp.), its consumption by children does not seem to be a risk factor of diarrhoea. In fact, the treatment of lettuce with Javel water before consumption appears to decrease the risk of transmission of the pathogenic microorganisms. However, lettuce can constitute transmission pathways for pathogenic bacteria such as *Salmonella* to consumers.

Women play a determining role in the treatment and sale of lettuce. Moreover, they are responsible for their households. Thus, it is essential to sensitize this population group on practices to adopt in order to minimize the risks of contamination at the market and in the household, one such practice being to disinfect the lettuce with chlorine prior to consumption.

Diarrhoea, as an indicator of the health status of a population, can have diverse origins (virus, parasites, and bacteria). Likewise, the contamination of groundwater can come from other diffuse or one-point sources, such as septic tanks, cemeteries, or the illicit dumping of wastewater. Thus, other studies will be required in order to distinguish the impact of urban agriculture from other risk factors that impact on the health of the surrounding populations.

Dissemination of results

At the end of our research project, a workshop allowed us to disseminate our preliminary results to the different stakeholders (researchers, public health department, farmers, and NGOs such as ENDA-RUP). We also participated in many conferences and published scientific articles.

Recommendations

Treatment of wastewater

The results of the study show that wastewater can constitute a good alternative on the condition that it is at least partially treated, i.e. that its bacterial and parasite load is reduced. Extensive treatment of wastewater with macrophytes, microphytes, or bare or planted gravel offer sustainable methods (Gaye and Niang, 2002) as they do not require electrical power and give satisfactory results. However, lack of space limits the degree to which such facilities can be established. In this context, small-scale treatment stations set up to implement a number of treatment steps and techniques (such as the pilot station of the wastewater treatment laboratory of IFAN, Université de Dakar) should be the preferred solution. The nutritional quality of wastewater for plants is very high. Moreover, its use will contribute to reducing the reliance of soil amendment by means of organic manure, in particular poultry manure.

Mode of irrigation

The mode of irrigation plays an important role in the contamination of vegetables, especially leafy vegetables (lettuce). For example, irrigating with watering cans can provoke the spread of microorganisms from the soil and the organic manure onto the vegetables, thereby promoting contamination. The fact that the polluted water from the watering cans comes into direct contact with the plants also leads to contamination. To minimize the microbiological pollution of vegetables, drip irrigation is strongly recommended, as this avoids contact of the irrigation water with the consumable parts of the plant. This mode of irrigation also allows reductions in water consumption.

Use of organic manure

The use of poultry manure constitutes a large risk, in particular for contamination with *Salmonella* sp. and *Campylobacter* sp. For the safe use of organic manure, co-composting is strongly recommended to eliminate pathogenic bacteria (Koné et al., 2007).

Disinfection of lettuce at home

The disinfection of vegetables, in particular lettuce, should be systematic in all households. In Senegal, the most widely used disinfectant is Javel water. However, the methods applied in households (dosage, reaction time) are not very efficient for bacterial elimination from the vegetables. A laboratory test showed that the efficient disinfection of vegetables requires one capsule of Javel water 8° (0.6 ml) per 10 litres of water (7.6 mg of chlorine per litre) and a contact time of 30 minutes in a hermetically sealed container (Javel water evaporates).

Disinfection of the groundwater before use

Water from wells and manual pumps that is used for domestic purposes (drinking and cooking water) must be filtered, heated, or disinfected with Javel. The SODIS method (solar water disinfection) developed by EAWAG (Switzerland) is an efficient method to disinfect small quantities of water intended for consumption using ultraviolet radiation from the sun (McGuigan et al., 1998; Méndez-Hermida et al., 2007). The technique is very simple and consists of putting clear water (not too turbid) in PET bottles and exposing them to sun rays for six hours. However, children, given their vulnerability, should ideally consume tap water or mineral water.

Future research

In the complex milieu of Niayes, other more rigorous research studies could lead to a better understanding of the issues and eventually allow the confirmation of certain hypotheses.

A molecular epidemiological study would allow for the confirmation of the different hypotheses and the identification of the different types of diarrhoea and microorganisms responsible. For example, molecular techniques such as lysotypy and rybotyping (Peduzzi, 1985; Peduzzi et al., 1991; Blanc and Siegrist, 1995), by which the source of the pathogenic strains can be distinguished (i.e. environmental source, such as water or vegetables, or from the stools of sick people), would facilitate the identification of cause–effect relationships.

Acknowledgements

This study was financed by the Swiss National Science Foundation (project no. 2070021-109689/1, category 'Partenariats avec les Pays du Sud') and the International Development Research Centre (IDRC) of Canada (ECOPOLIS grant no. 103710-99906060-004).

References

Al-Lahham, O., El Assi, N. M., and Fayyad, M. (2003) 'Impact of treated waste-water irrigation on quality attributes and contamination of tomato fruit', *Agricultural Water Management* 61(1): 51–62.

Amoah, P., Drechsel, P., and Abaidoo, R. C. (2005) 'Irrigated urban vegetable production in Ghana: Sources of pathogen contamination and health risk elimination', *Irrigation and Drainage* 54(S1): S49–S61.

ANSD (Agence Nationale de la statistique et de la démographie) (2007) 'Situation économique et sociale de la région de Dakar en 2006: Service régional de la statistique et de la démographie de Dakar', Agence Nationale de la statistique et de la démographie, Dakar.

Assemblée Nationale (1983) *Code de l'hygiène: Act no. 8371*, 5 July, Assemblée Nationale, Dakar.

Baldé, D. (2005) 'Providing the city with fresh vegetables from urban and peri-urban spaces. Social and economical benefits and constraints, impacts on public health: The case of Patte d'Oie', Commune of Dakar, Dakar.

Beuchat, L. R. (1998) 'Surface decontamination of fruits and vegetables eaten raw: A review. Food safety issues', WHO/FSF/FOS/98.2, Food Safety Unit, WHO, USA.

Blanc, D. S. and Siegrist, H.-R. (1995) 'Type bactérien: méthodes et valeur épidémiologique', *Swiss-NOSO* 2(1), www.swissnoso.ch/fr/bulletin/articles/article/typage-bacterien-methodes-et-valeur-epidemiologique [accessed 28 September 2011].

Bolster, C. H., Walker, S. L., and Cook, K. L. (2006) 'Comparison of *Escherichia coli* and *Campylobacter jejuni* transport in saturated porous media', *J. Environ. Qual.* 35(4): 1018–25.

DPS (Direction de la Prévision et de la statistique) (2003) *Situation économique et sociale du Sénégal*, Ministry of the Economy and Finance of the Republic of Senegal, Dakar.

Ensink, J. H. J., Van der Hoek, W., Matsuno, Y., Munir, S., and Aslam, M. R. (2002) *Use of Untreated Wastewater in Peri-urban Agriculture in Pakistan: Risks and Opportunities*, International Water Management Institute. Report no. 64. Colombo, Sri Lanka.

Faruqui, N., Niang, S., and Redwood, M. (2004) 'Untreated wastewater reuse in market gardens: A case study of Dakar, Senegal', in C. A. Scott, N. I. Faruqui , and L. Raschid-Sally (eds) *Wastewater Use in Irrigated Agriculture: Confronting the Livelihood and Environmental Realities*, pp. 1113–25, Wallingford, CAB International in association with the International Water Management Institute and IDRC.

Gagneux, S., Schneider, C., Odermatt, O., Cissé, G., Dah, O. C., Lemine, O. M. S., Touré, A., and Tanner, M. (1999) 'La diarrhée chez les agriculteurs urbains de Nouakchott en Mauritanie', *Med. Trop.*, 59: 253–8.

Gaye, M. and Niang, S. (2002) 'Epuration extensive des eaux usées pour leur réutilisation dans l'agriculture urbaine: des technologies appropriées en zone sahélienne pour la lutte contre la pauvreté', Etudes et recherches 225–7, ENDA, Dakar.

Hussain, I., Raschid, L., Hanjra, M. A., Marikar, F., and Van der Hoek, W. (2002) 'Wastewater use in agriculture: Review of impacts and methodological issues in valuing impacts' (with an extended list of bibliographical references), IWMI working paper 37, International Water Management Institute, Colombo, Sri Lanka.

Ibenyassine, K., AitMhand, R., Karamoko, Y., Cohen, N., and Ennaji, M. M. (2006) 'Use of repetitive DNA sequences to determine the persistence of enteropathogenic *Escherichia coli* in vegetables and in soil grown in fields treated with contaminated irrigation water', *Letters in Applied Microbiology* 43(5): 528–33.

ICMSF (International Commission for Microbiological Specifications for Foods) (1986) *Microorganisms in Foods 2. Sampling for Microbiological Analysis: Principles and Specific Applications. International Commission for Microbiological Specifications for Foods*, vol. 2, Blackwell Scientific Publications, Oxford.

Kone, D., Coffie, C., Zurbrügg, C., Gallizzia, K., Mosera, D., Dreschera, S., and Strauss, M. (2007) 'Helminth eggs inactivation efficiency by faecal sludge dewatering and co-composting in tropical climates', *Water Research* 41: 4397–402.

Lampel, K. A., Orlandi, P. A., and Kornegay, L. (2000) 'Improved template preparation for PCR-based assays for detection of food-borne bacterial pathogens', *Appl. Environ. Microbiol.* 66(10): 4539–42.

Majdoub, R., Côté, C., Labidi, M., Guay, K., and Généreux, M. (2003) *Impact de l'utilisation des engrais de ferme sur la qualité microbiologique de l'eau souterraine*, Institut de recherche et de développement en agroenvironnement, Quebec.

Mayer, R. and Ouellet, F. (1991) *Méthodologie de recherches pour les intervenants sociaux*, Edition Gaëtan Morin, Quebec.

Mbaye, A. (1999) 'Production des légumes à Dakar: Importance, contraintes et potentialités', in O. Smith (ed.) *Agriculture urbaine en Afrique de l'ouest*, ed., pp. 56–66, IDRC, Ottawa.

McGuigan, K. G. Joice, T. M., Conroy, R. M, Gillespie, J., and Elmore-Meegan, M. (1998) 'Solar disinfection of drinking water contained in transparent plastic bottles: Characterizing the bacterial inactivation process', *Journal of Applied Microbiology* 84(6): 1138–48.

Melloul, A. A. and Hassani, L. (1999) 'Salmonella infection in children from the wastewater-spreading zone of Marrakesh city (Morocco)', *Journal of Applied Microbiology* 87(4): 536–9.

Méndez-Hermida, F., Ares-Mazás, E., McGuigan, K. G., Boyle, M., Sichel, C., and Fernández-Ibáñez, P. (2007) 'Disinfection of drinking water contaminated with *Cryptosporidium parvum* oocysts under natural sunlight and using the photocatalyst TiO_2', *Journal of Photochemistry and Photobiology B: Biology* 88(2–3): 105–11.

Mensah, P. (2005) 'Surveillance et suivi des maladies d'origine alimentaire dans le contrôle alimentaire', WHO Regional Office for Africa, ftp://ftp.fao.org/es/esn/food/meetings/2005/italy_pres6_fr.pdf [accessed 12 December 2009].

Ndiaye, M. L. (2009) 'Impacts sanitaires des eaux d'arrosage de l'agriculture urbaine de Dakar (Sénégal)', Doctoral thesis no. 4110, Faculty of Sciences, Université de Genève, Geneva.

Niang, S. (2002) 'Maîtrise des risques dans la valorisation des eaux usées en agriculture urbaine', in Fall, S.T., Akinbamijo, O.O. and Smith, O. B. (eds) *Advances in Crop-livestock Integration in West African Cities*, pp. 101–16, ITC, Banjul (Gambia); ISRA, Dakar; IDRC, Ottawa.

OECD (Organisation for Economic Co-operation and Development) (2003) *Assessing Microbial Safety of Drinking Water: Improving Approaches and Methods*, IWA Publishing, London.

Peduzzi, R. (1985) 'Pollution aquatique, microbiologie et pathologie humaine', *Méd. et Hyg.* 43: 3485–8.

Peduzzi, R., Demarta, A., and Poloni, C. (1991) 'Pathologie microbiennes d'origine hydrique', *Méd. et Hyg.* 49: 3455–6.

Prüss-Üstün, A., Bos, R., Gore, F., and Bartram, J. (2008) *Safer Water, Better Health: Costs, Benefits and Sustainability of Interventions to Protect and Promote Health*, World Health Organization, Geneva.

Rosas, I., Baez, A., and Coutino, M. (1984) 'Bacteriological quality of crops irrigated with wastewater in the Xochimilco plots, Mexico City, Mexico', *Appl. Environ. Microbiol.* 47(5): 1074–9.

Smith, O. B. (2002) 'Overview of urban agriculture and food security in West African cities', in S. T. Fall, O. O. Akinbamijo and O. B. Smith (eds) *Advances in Crop-livestock Integration in West African Cities*, pp. 17–36, ITC, Banjul (Gambia); ISRA, Dakar; IDRC, Ottawa.

Trang, D. T., Hien, B. T. T., Mølbak, K., Cam, P. D., and Dalsgaard, A. (2007) 'Epidemiology and aetiology of diarrhoeal diseases in adults engaged in wastewater-fed agriculture and aquaculture in Hanoi, Vietnam', *Tropical Medicine and International Health* 12 (s2): 23–33.

UN-Water (2006) *Coping with Water Scarcity: A Strategic Issue and Priority for System-wide Action*, UN-Water, FAO, Rome.

Van der Hoek, W., Hassan, M. U., Ensink, J. H. J., Feenstra, S., Raschid-Sally, L., Munir, S., Aslam, R., Ali, N., Hussain, R., and Matsuno, Y. (2002) *Urban Wastewater: A Valuable Resource for Agriculture. A Case Study from Haroonabad, Pakistan*, International Water Management Institute, Report no. 63. Colombo, Sri Lanka.

WHO (2006) *Guidelines for Drinking-water Quality: Incorporating First Addendum to Third Edition*, vol. 1, Recommendations, 3rd edition, WHO, Geneva.

About the author

Mamadou Lamine Ndiaye is an independent consultant currently working for the microbiology group of Medicago Inc., Quebec City, Canada. He holds a master's degree in biophysics as well as master's and doctoral degrees in environmental sciences from the University of Geneva, Switzerland. He has worked on the issue of wastewater reuse in urban agriculture, including its impacts on groundwater pollution, the quality of vegetables, and human health.

Chapter 3

Participatory transformation of the Women's Centre of Malika, Senegal: Strategies for the development of a productive ecosystem in the peri-urban context

Émilie Pinard

Abstract

This action-research project examines how structural building design can become a catalyst in the participation of women in local governance and ecological practices. The project involved the transformation and expansion of an existing building – the Women's Centre in Malika, a suburb of Dakar, Senegal – in order to integrate productive practices such as urban agriculture. It also involved the redesign of the surrounding compound into an ecological system capable of efficiently recycling water and solid waste, limiting energy consumption, and maximizing the health and well-being of its users. The project draws from three approaches: integrated planning, participatory design processes, and analysis of the built environment and local governance from the perspective of women. The project also promoted means by which to ensure the dissemination of acquired skills.

Introduction

More than one half of the world's population now lives in cities. Urbanization is especially rampant in the Global South, particularly in Africa (UNFPA, 2007). The uncontrolled expansion of African cities into rural and agricultural areas contributes to the disappearance of arable land – land that could serve to feed city dwellers in a sustainable manner. The residential neighbourhoods created by this urban expansion generally lack basic infrastructure such as streets, and essential services such as potable water, electricity, and sanitary waste management. Malika, a territory located at the periphery of Dakar, is representative of this phenomenon.

Situated at the rural–urban interface, Malika has traditionally been a food producer. Small-scale agriculture is practised in the form of domestic livestock farming and vegetable gardening, on lots temporarily left abandoned. Run and operated mainly by women, these farms and gardens allow participants to achieve a higher standard of food security for themselves and their families (Mougeot, 2006). However, small-scale agriculture is threatened by land tenure insecurity and is generally carried out in built environments that are poorly suited for it, with subsequent negative impacts on the environment and the sanitary conditions of nearby living quarters. The Pikine Department, where Malika is located, has the highest number of poor households and the lowest income levels in all of Senegal, along with a significant amount of informal economic activity (Minvielle et al., 2000). With most households already having to spend up to 80 per cent of their budgets on food (Mougeot, 2006), recent price hikes have resulted in fewer and fewer people being able to meet their food needs, significantly impacting on the population's health and ability to study and work. According to a survey conducted in Diamalaye, an informal settlement within Malika, the difficulty to feed one's own household is considered to be the principal sign of poverty (IAGU, 2007).

Objectives and research questions

It is within this context that this project for the development, improvement, and promotion of small-scale agriculture and construction practices was mounted and given support from IDRC's Ecopolis research and design grant. The choice of topics was determined on the basis of the context of the poverty, household needs, and community resources. The Women's Centre of Malika seemed to be highly suited as a focal point for the project. It is housed in a community building that is well known to the population and where the women are already engaged in activities related to food, income generation, and education. The structure of the building was maladapted, in terms of both space and layout, to the actual needs and cultural practices of its users, which hindered the diversification of activities, in turn impeding the attraction of new members. The objective of our project was to help the women integrate their community centre into urban agriculture and to encourage their participation in the realization of architectural transformations of the building. These measures sought to allow the women to generate new sources of food and income, experiment with new forms of productive activities, and train other women and teenage girls so that they could adopt the acquired practices in their own place of habitation.

We focused our work on two interrelated areas of research and action: the development of architectural layouts and arrangements as well as measures for integrating agriculture into the lot, existing buildings, and new buildings; and the participation in and management of productive activities by women. Our main questions were the following: How could we design the architectural transformations and new constructions so that they would be supportive of existing cultural practices and integrate the practice of urban agriculture? What were the most accessible measures for promoting the integration of urban agriculture into the built environment and for optimizing the use of available resources? What were the most effective participatory methods for encouraging the members of the Women's Centre to take charge of new productive activities? These challenges called on us to examine how urban agriculture and the built environment interact with each other. The project thus engaged with the spatial planning of the compound as much as with the building itself, including its roofs, walls, fences, and annexes.

Theoretical framework

Two main hypotheses, or premises, guided our action-research process. The first is that the compound, and its neighbourhood, should be understood as a productive ecosystem that should recycle water and waste as best as possible, keep energy expenditures at a minimum, and maximize the health and comfort of its inhabitants. This means that the design of the compound as a whole, the buildings, and the various adaptations, should be based on integrated and ecological planning principles. The site and the collective were viewed as having the necessary resources and capacity to engage in agricultural production, provided that secondary products such as waste and wastewater could be recycled as best as possible. The implemented urban agriculture would then use and reuse the resources available from within the compound (Moustier and Fall, 2004). When practised at the scale of the compound, urban agriculture can promote the preservation of the natural environment, the improvement of the living environment, and the reduction of the vulnerability of poor households by contributing to their income, food security, and health of members (Temple and Moustier, 2004; Broutin et al., 2005). In this way, urban agriculture is among the strategies for mitigating the consequences of exceedingly rapid urban growth (Mougeot, 2006).

The second hypothesis is that a gradual and participatory process of design and implementation leads to the production of built forms that are culturally adapted, while improving participants' understanding and acceptance of the required changes with regard to the natural and built environment. The project was inspired by a body of research that focuses on the process of design and technological innovation. This kind of research strives, among other aims, to get specialists from different disciplines to work together and to put the practices and know-how of users at the centre of research. Such knowledge sharing in the early design stage has proven to be particularly useful when researching the built environment, which spans multiple disciplines and comprises diverse functions and impacts (Sanoff, 2000).

This hypothesis also takes into account the research on the relationships between men and women and, in particular, the condition of women. Feminist analyses of urban planning and the living environment strive to meet the particular needs of women and, above all, to question the division of gender roles (Moser, 1993; Hainard and Verschuur, 2001). Studies on the transformations of the Senegalese habitat (Osmont, 1980; Tall, 2009) have allowed us to recognize the value of certain spatial elements of traditional Senegalese architecture that had fallen out of use with the onset of modernist constructions, such as the Women's Centre. Such elements include the distribution of rooms, the allocation of rooms, and the relationship between courtyard and living unit or between open and closed spaces (Osmont, 1980). The courtyard as 'living room' for the community as a whole to receive visitors, prepare meals, or pray has practically disappeared since the Women's Centre was built in the middle of the site (Photo 3.1). However, the exterior courtyard is used to prepare meals by the women of the Women's Centre. Using the centre's kitchen more as a junk room, they prefer to prepare meals outside, as is traditional custom, in a space that is ventilated, large, and offers a view onto the courtyard.

The project thus contributes to each of the cited fields of knowledge by examining the built living environment, still under-researched in connection with urban agriculture and integrated planning (see Viljoen, 2005, and Bhatt, 2006, for the first works on the subject). The objective was to adapt and explore the methods of participatory design and interdisciplinary collaborations in the Senegalese context by engaging the women in the spatial and material design of the built living environment – an activity from which women have traditionally been excluded and that has been largely neglected as a topic of research in projects addressing women.

Émilie Pinard

Photo 3.1 Panoramic views of the terrain of the Women's Centre of Malika, prior to the project

Approach

The project is part of a series of collaborations between the group Habitats et cultures of Université Laval, the Institut Africain de Gestion Urbaine (IAGU), and the collective of Malika. These collaborations, underway since September 2007, concern the Mbeubeuss landfill and the living environment and natural environment of the suburbs of Dakar (IAGU, 2006; Casault et al., 2007, 2008). As the participation of women, the community, and the various local actors are essential elements for developing appropriate solutions in action research of this type, collective decision-making informed and determined many aspects of this project, be it with regard to construction, training, or the spread of the project. In that context, a monitoring committee, composed of 10 women, was created to monitor the project from beginning to end and to assign and share responsibilities. The committee benefited from the expertise, support, and contacts of different researchers/collaborators associated with the project, namely: the personnel of the IAGU; Seydou Niang of the Laboratoire de traitement des eaux usées of IFAN at Université Cheikh Anta Diop; Youga Niang of the Centre pour le développement de l'horticulture (CDH); Ayao Missohou of the École Inter-États des Sciences et Médecine Vétérinaires (EISMV) of Université Cheikh Anta Diop of Dakar; and M. Nabi Kane of the Collège d'architecture de Dakar.

During a preceding internship at the IAGU, I managed a participatory design project on the possibilities of expanding and transforming the Women's Centre of Malika. The data for this project were collected by the following means: an evaluation of the building, conducted in a participatory manner by the women; photo documentation on the modes of occupation, the work of the women, and the material conditions of the site and the building; and visits and analyses of other women's centres in Senegal. Based on those data, the Women's Centre in Malika was found to be poorly adapted (concerning materials, work spaces, circulation on the site, safety, etc.) and lacking with regard to its environmental performance and its ability to respond to the needs and cultural practices of the women (Photo 3.2). The women members and I thus developed an architectural transformation programme, to be implemented over time, to the end of building capacity and diversifying their practices and collective know-how (e.g. micro-gardens, domestic livestock production). The aim of the action research presented in this study was to advance the debate and understanding begun with that project and realize some of the planned transformations for integrating agricultural practices within the compound.

The research phase of the project was dedicated to deepening knowledge on the subject and to validating the work of the preceding stages. The aim was essentially to review the objectives and priorities of the Women's Centre that had been determined in prior design proposals, in order to ensure that these could satisfy the technical and financial constraints imposed by the current project. One of the first activities realized with the monitoring committee and the other members of the centre was to determine which interventions

Émilie Pinard

Photo 3.2 The occupation of space: Food preparation

should be carried out in the built environment. The selected interventions consisted of the following activities: providing access to the roof so that it could be used as a terrace; setting up semi-exterior spaces for activities of food preparation and dyeing; and increasing the safety and visibility of the house. In parallel, a study was conducted on the different technologies used in urban agriculture and their potential integration into the design project. This then allowed us to identify diverse techniques that were appropriate for our project and to determine the optimal space requirements and light conditions for their application.

Following these first studies, the project's design and preparation for implementation were further developed by examining the different factors concerning the construction process (e.g. contractor and labour, appropriate methods, availability of materials, and building inspection) and developing the architectural and structural drawings (Figure 3.1). After a review of the design by the monitoring committee, a call for offers was distributed to local contractors for the execution of the masonry and plumbing. The decision to handle finishing works such as tiling, painting, or the installation of doors ourselves was made in preparatory meetings held at the construction site. It was based on a compromise between, on the one hand, wanting to make the most of a limited budget and promoting learning by engaging people from the community for certain works, and, on the other hand, the importance of

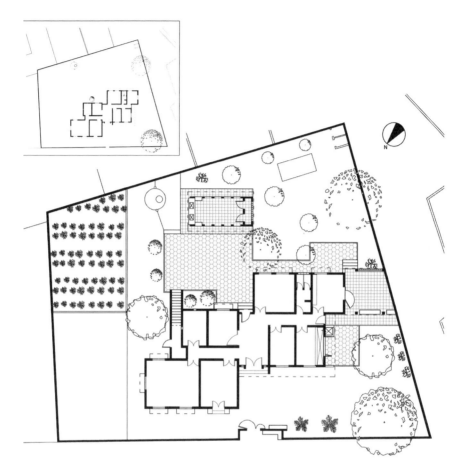

Figure 3.1 Floor plan, before and after, of the different constructions and changes
made to the site

Source: Émilie Pinard

getting construction tasks accomplished by competent professionals, which
also serves to support the construction trades, which are often left out in
small-budget constructions.

The last stage of the project consisted of a collaboration between the
contractor, the workers, the researchers, and other women and teenage girls
from the centre to execute the actual construction and to set up the different
urban agriculture tools and systems. During this stage, the monitoring
committee, in addition to its weekly meetings to monitor progress and to
plan training, held update and consultation meetings with the other members
of the centre. These meetings allowed us to listen to criticism, concerns, and
requests, to explain our choices, and also to receive recognition for our work.

Representation tools, such as photomontages, proved to be very useful to facilitate the visualization of the work and the expected final result (Photo 3.3). The work – the pace of which increased significantly towards the end of the construction, thanks to the participation of the women in various finishing and agricultural tasks – was concluded with a qualitative evaluation of the process and a search for means to disseminate the acquired skills and knowledge.

Results

The architectural transformations were designed and realized with the aim of providing support and protection for the diverse productive practices. Simple modifications were first made to the existing building, such as to adapt it better to the needs and activities of the women and to improve its thermal comfort.

Openings in the outside walls of the building were created to increase the number of access points to specific areas of the site. The addition of a door in the back of the building gave access to a part of the site that had been left unexploited until then, while also favouring cross ventilation inside the building. And, an opening of the existing kitchen towards the outside facilitated the transportation of materials and improved light and aeration in a variety of spaces (interior, semi-covered, exterior). The roof terrace was also adapted for gardening activities, and a staircase was built to access it.

The enclosure wall was transformed to create an entry portal that was more welcoming and above all more visible from the street. The integrated benches

Photo 3.3 Photomontage of the semi-exterior kitchen built and occupied by the women

Émilie Pinard and Jean-Philippe Saucier

on both sides of the wall now merge with the public space and offer a shaded resting place for mornings and afternoons. A new metal door also safeguards the plants and various belongings of the centre.

The ground around the building was redeveloped according to the types of activity foreseen. This task enabled the protection of zones dedicated to cultivation and offers outside work spaces, in keeping with the layout of traditional domestic courtyards. Well demarcated, they are designed to decrease the risks of contamination and the mingling of activities that are incompatible.

Small annex buildings were constructed, with the aim of promoting the densification of the site while at the same time recreating an interior courtyard. Our goal was to design healthy and adapted construction models according to architectural principles that could be easily reproduced in houses and other small public buildings.

These annexes included a covered but largely aerated area, designated mainly for dyeing, and accompanied by a cesspool to gather wastewater (Photo 3.4). The concrete is protected from direct sunlight by a slightly raised fibre cement roof, which ensures the space is cool, even in the afternoons.

A further annex consists of a semi-exterior kitchen that serves as an extension of the interior spaces for food preparation (see Photo 3.3). This annex

Émilie Pinard

Photo 3.4   Annex built for dyeing activities

allows women to continue cooking outside while benefiting from a ventilated and shady space. The sanitary working conditions were improved with
ceramic surfaces, as well as with benches and a wall made of Claustra, reducing
the amount of wind and dust at ground level without blocking the views.

Different urban agriculture tools or techniques were then implemented on
the site, based on diverse experimental and agricultural approaches, in order
to be able to measure and compare results.

The type of micro-gardening system introduced by this project in the
Senegalese communities is that of 'planting tables', which are wooden tables
lined with plastic. Thanks to the many training programmes for this kind
of gardening, and their low cost, it is easy to obtain support to launch such
systems. Some members of the centre had participated in training and then
used their connections to secure further material from those programmes.
At the very beginning of the project, the women built new planting tables,
the yield and efficacy of which we then observed. Once the roof works were
finished, we installed the micro-gardens on the roofs (Photo 3.5). These
gardening systems also serve to keep sunlight from directly hitting the surface
of the roof. Made of concrete, these roofs normally accumulate heat easily;
however, with a micro-garden, they remain cool. This considerably increases
thermal comfort inside the building.

For wastewater management, the project took into account the well and
the discharge of water used for dyeing. The centre's well is the main source of
water supply for the women and for some families from the vicinity. Unlike
the potable water provided by the municipality, the well water is free. This is

Émilie Pinard

Photo 3.5 Micro-gardens on the roof of the centre

what allowed the women to perform their many high-water-use activities, as well as to offer the well water to neighbours in exchange for labour. The water also proved to be safe, with a water analysis showing that it contained no hazardous metals. We were thus able to use the water for the activities of the centre, provided, of course, we ensured the maintenance of its quality. We also had to determine how we were going to manage the wastewater of the new dye house. The most accessible and safest solution was to connect the wash basins and a floor drain to a good-sized, watertight cesspool, to which the dye water could be discharged and stored (Photo 3.6). For the women, this cesspool served to raise awareness of the importance of wastewater management and the maintenance of water quality for agricultural activities.

Fruit trees are an obviously promising form of urban agriculture. They are not very expensive in Senegal and require little technology or maintenance. Our first drafts of the development plan thus already foresaw a zone where diverse species of fruit trees could be planted. Certain climbing plants would be planted close to openwork walls, while other more imposing plants would serve as the main source of shade on the site. When the construction was fairly advanced, allowing us to free up and clean the ground, we had a 'planting day' on which we planted 10 species of fruit trees, accompanied by a training session on their maintenance and watering.

Émilie Pinard

Photo 3.6 The wash basins of the building connected to a watertight cesspool

Some of the women from the centre had done workshops on composting and on an intensive gardening technique called *le centième d'hectare* (a hundredth of a hectare). This technique, the main objective of which is to make an urban space profitable on the basis of the demand for and scarce supply of certain fruits and vegetables, is practised on a piece of land measuring 10 m^2. It makes use of compost obtained from the recuperation of various kinds of manures and domestic waste. The learning process, which was very practice-oriented, was greatly appreciated by the women, who declared that they intended to apply the acquired skills at various places in the city. We also designated a parcel of land to this form of agriculture at the centre.

We were inspired by a plant container model developed by the Montreal-based NGO Alternatives to manufacture growers from recycled materials. The system is produced using old buckets and pipes and is thus not very costly. However, it nevertheless proved to be the most challenging and experimental kind of system in the sense that the local population were not familiar with it and that the set-up was more technical and complex than it first seemed. The system can also be expected to require future adaptations.

Discussion and lessons learned

This action research raises questions concerning the long-term sustainability of development and capacity-building projects. Most projects do not consider certain working skills as being components of a broader structure; nor do they recognize that productive activities such as urban agriculture require capacity with regard to managing time, skills, and costs. As a result, such capacities are often lacking, being neither required as prerequisites prior to the start of projects nor deliberately developed during projects. These findings coincide with our experiences with the micro-garden programme in Senegal, and are also consistent with findings by Broutin et al. (2005) on the analysis of diverse forms of urban agriculture in Thiès, Senegal.

The training programme, supported by the Ministère de l'Agriculture and the FAO, lasts several days and provides women with materials and a basic understanding of the table planter technique. Fertilizers and seeds are available only for as long as the programme offers them free of charge. The learning period is of a short duration, leaving participants little time to assimilate the amount of practical and theoretical knowledge transmitted, and the results are not long-lasting. Broutin et al. (2005) estimate that a table planter is good for three years' cultivation. Moreover, we found that the programme took little account of the context in which the planters are implemented. For example, major factors such as site planning and a site's resources or its built environment are often neglected. The poor mix of concrete used for roofs and its lack of watertightness turned out to be a major obstacle in the implementation of the system, as water was constantly dripping from the roof. Nevertheless, given that the system can exploit rooftop terraces, it is often presented as a viable solution to the lack of space in the city (FAO, 2002). This raises questions concerning the value of micro-gardening using table planters for neighbourhoods, of which there are many, in which the roofs of most houses are poorly constructed and made with poor quality concrete. Thus, although urban agriculture is supposed to be very simple and inexpensive, it does have disadvantages over the long term when applied to poorly built concrete housing.

A multifunctional design

In our project, by contrast, we favoured an integrative ecosystemic approach, in which waste management, the recovery and treatment of wastewater, and the production of food are (re)integrated into the compounds and neighbourhoods. Rather than viewing the built environment as a mere accessory, we see it as the core of the system. The approach envisions new constructions that support productive activities and agriculture, considers possible future expansion, and ensures that the gardening zones are well defined and above all protected. In this way, urban agriculture can become a component of the site rather than an isolated tool. Food security, health, and environmental and sanitary degradation all become principal parameters in the design and construction of urban planning projects alongside the conventional economic or material constraints.

Moreover, in our approach, urban agriculture infrastructures or measures are not implemented without first taking into account the quality of the site and the new constructions, as these determine the space occupancy and productivity of the new systems. This led us to engage in the improvement of local construction practices, both with regard to the techniques employed and the selection of planning principles likely to offer a better living environment. In this respect, we sought to revive many of Senegal's traditional construction practices, including basic elements concerning natural ventilation or protection from the sun, techniques that had fallen out of use following the rapid introduction of Western models of construction and materials. In collaborating with the local builders, who are generally not involved in development projects, we evaluated the impacts of the use of concrete, today the most widespread construction material in Senegal. Our aim here was to effectively exploit the characteristics of concrete (e.g. its thermal mass, structural capacity, and uniformity of surfaces) in order to create spaces that are better adapted to the climate and to conventional practices.

Learning by doing

Our action- and practice-oriented method proved to be very efficient in allowing participants to learn new approaches to planning and architecture. The project was thus a fruitful experience in many respects for the builders as well as for the women members of the committee. For example, the training for laying the ceramic tiles on the benches and low walls allowed the women to replicate this task at the domestic scale, or at least to oversee its implementation. In fact, several weeks after the training, during the work supervision phase, they were still able to remember relatively complex aspects of the preparatory stages of this work.

Unfortunately, the assimilation of knowledge and skills was not as successful with regard to the urban agriculture measures, which were realized later than planned in the project. It was not until a monitoring committee was formed and consolidated that a new urban agriculture committee could be set up, composed of a former and little active micro-gardening committee as well as some members of the monitoring committee. This left very little time to evaluate and modify the maintenance and work procedures, and even less time to make a comparative assessment of the gardening activities.

Post-project follow-up

We found the means to ensure the spread and reproduction of the acquired skills begun during the project. However, ongoing guidance of sorts, mainly with regard to the structure of the research teams and the management of the products, remains necessary so that the efforts so far deployed will pay off. For example, the new urban agriculture committee had little experience on which to build, and the short training which its members received did not address issues concerning team work or the coordination of schedules and tasks for a group of workers. We hope that other partner organizations seeking to apply this field of knowledge will be able to contribute to the pursuit of this research design. For example, interns specialized in organizational aspects of urban agriculture could, under the aegis of those organizations, work with the women on the implementation of management tools that are adapted to their needs. This would allow the interns to evaluate the diverse techniques that were explored during the project.

To promote a broader dissemination of results, the Senegalese NGO Bibliothèque-Lecture-Développement, in collaboration with the group Habitats et culture, the IAGU, and the project's monitoring committee are, inspired by this experience, preparing the publication of a documentary album for children. The album will present simple, easily reproducible, and inexpensive interventions that can transform a typical house from informal housing compounds of African cities into 'house gardens'. We look forward to the publication of this album and believe that it will educate children and, through them, the members of their families in the ways in which urban houses and habitats can be adapted to climate change.

Recommendations

This research complements the ever-growing list of studies on integrating urban agriculture into cities and dwellings, as discussed in an editorial in the journal *Open House International* (Bhatt and Farah, 2009). Many of the planning principles and measures presented here can be adapted to other settings, provided the specific context of their implementation is taken into consideration. This project illustrates the important role that city dwellers and local decision-makers play in making urban agriculture a productive, long-term, and profitable activity, from both the human and ecological standpoints. To maximize this role, we recommend intervention measures at two levels: a modification of local training programmes; and, a review of real estate and land use policies that are likely to promote an ecosystemic planning approach.

Local training programmes should focus more on teaching advanced, practical skills, in order to encourage the professionalization of the sectors affiliated with urban agriculture. Theory-based training seminars (generally given by women) do exist in Dakar, on topics including micro-gardening, dyeing, food processing, and poultry breeding. However, as discussed in the context of micro-gardening, these programmes are usually not sustainable over the long term. The collaborative approach taken during this project, focusing on concrete problems and solutions that can be implemented on site by the participating women, appeared to yield the most promising results. In such a context, members of the centre can become trainers for other women's groups, spreading the theoretical and practical knowledge they acquired during the project. From a more global perspective, we believe that training programmes should address a wide range of issues surrounding urban agriculture (e.g. marketing, transformation, and partnership) and its associated activities (e.g. planning, construction, and remediation). This finding is consistent with those of other on-site studies in Senegal (IAGU, 2004; Cissé et al., 2005).

The results of this research and design project show that an ecosystemic approach to planning – in other words, a better integration of the diverse resources of the site and of waste management – does in fact lend itself to application at the neighbourhood scale. In the context of increasing competition for space, agricultural land is often lost to residential buildings and infrastructure. Real estate and land use policies should not only seek to limit those losses, but also to integrate ecological systems into existing neighbourhoods, making urban agriculture an integral part of the city. In addition to providing economic advantages, urban agriculture also contributes to limiting energy expenditures for buildings, improving the comfort of inhabitants, and providing the ability to reuse or process diverse forms of waste. The conditions under which such policies could be implemented and respected must also be examined. By pursuing research on urbanization from this ecosystemic perspective, we will be in a better position to understand the role of urban agriculture in the economies of cities, the health of their inhabitants, and the global fight against the harmful effects of climate change.

Acknowledgements

For this research, I benefited from an Écopolis grant from IDRC, Ottawa, Canada. I thank all researchers and collaborators involved in the project: the staff of the IAGU, as well as Seydou Niang, Youga Niang, Ayao Missohou, M. Nabi Kane; the personnel and the students of the Collège d'architecture de Dakar; and the staff of Bibliothèque-Lecture-Développement. I also thank the team of the group Habitats et cultures of the School of Architecture of Université Laval for its support: professors André Casault, Denise Piché, and Louise Lachapelle, and students Jessica Gagnon, Geneviève Reid, Simon Pelletier, and Jean-Philippe Saucier. Finally, I wish to highlight the contribution of the members of the Women's Centre of Malika, and thank in particular the project's monitoring committee for its dedication: Fatou Diop, Aïda Fall, Aissatou Diène, Awa Mbaye, Khadi Diop, Khoudia Sow, Kiné Bé, Mariatou Dieng, and Sabine Sarr.

References

Bhatt, V. (2006) *Making the Edible Landscape: Narrative Report*, McGill University, Montreal.
Bhatt, V. and Farah, L. M. (2009) 'Designing edible landscapes', *Open House International* 34(2): 5–7.
Broutin C., Commeat P.-G., and Sokona K. (2005) 'Le maraîchage face aux contraintes et opportunités de l'expansion urbaine. Le cas de Thiès/Fandène (Sénégal)', Ecocité working document no. 2. GRET/ENDA GRAF, Dakar.
Casault, A., Lachapelle, L., and Piché, D. (2007) 'Charrette participative à Dakar: L'intégration des pratiques d'agriculture urbaine à l'architecture, au design urbain et à l'aménagement des quartiers populaires de Dakar au Sénégal', Grant application, École d'architecture, Université Laval, Quebec.
Casault, A., Lachapelle, L., and Piché, D. (2008) 'Vers une collectivité productive à Malika (Sénégal): une expérience d'aménagement participatif', Grant application, École d'architecture, Université Laval, Quebec.
Cissé O., Diop Gueye, N. F., and Sy, M. (2005) 'Institutional and legal aspects of urban agriculture in French-speaking West Africa: From marginalization to legitimization', *Environment & Urbanization* 17(1): 143–54.
FAO (Food and Agriculture Organization of the United Nations) (2002) 'Les jardins urbains peuvent-ils aider à nourrir les villes surpeuplées?', www.fao.org/nouvelle/2002/020102-f.htm [accessed 4 March 2010].
Hainard, F. and Verschuur, C. (eds) (2001) *Femmes dans les crises urbaines. Relations de genre et environnements précaires*, Éditions Karthala, Paris.
IAGU (Institut Africain de Gestion Urbaine) (2004) 'Genre et agriculture urbaine dans la vallée des Niayes de Pikine (Sénégal)', exploratory case study, IAGU/RUAF, Dakar.
IAGU (2006) 'Décharge de Mbeubeuss: Analyse des impacts et amélioration des conditions de vie et de l'environnement à Diamalaye (Malika), Dakar', detailed proposition, IAGU, Dakar.

IAGU (2007) 'Enquête socio-économique de Diamalaye: Rapport d'analyse', IAGU, Dakar.

Minvielle, J. P., Diop, A., and Niang, A. (2000) *La pauvreté au Sénégal. Des statistiques à la réalité*, Éditions Karthala, Paris.

Moser, C. (1993) *Gender Planning and Development. Theory, Practice and Training*, Routledge, New York.

Mougeot, L. J. A. (2006) *Cultiver de meilleures villes. Agriculture urbaine et développement durable*, International Development Research Centre (IDRC), Ottawa.

Moustier, P. and Fall. A. S. (2004) 'Les dynamiques de l'agriculture urbaine: Caractérisation et évaluation' in Smith O. B., Moustier, P., Mougeot L. J. A., and Fall, A. (eds) (2004) *Développement durable de l'agriculture urbaine en Afrique francophone. Enjeux, concepts et méthods*, pp. 23–43, International Development Research Centre (IDRC), Ottawa.

Osmont, A. (1980) 'Modèles culturels et habitat. Études de cas à Dakar', *Anthropologie et Sociétés* 4(1): 97–114.

Sanoff, H. (2000) *Community Participation Methods in Design and Planning*, John Wiley & Sons, New York.

Tall, S. M. (2009) *Investir dans la ville africaine. Les émigrés et l'habitat à Dakar*, Éditions Karthala, Paris.

Temple, L. and Moustier, P. (2004) 'Les fonctions et contraintes de l'agriculture urbaine dans quelques villes africaines (Yaoundé, Cotonou, Dakar)', *Cahiers agricultures* 13: 15–22.

UNFPA (United Nations Population Fund) (2007) *État de la population mondiale 2007: Libérer le potentiel de la croissance urbaine*, United Nations Population Fund, New York.

Viljoen, A. (ed.) (2005) *CPULs: Continuous Productive Urban Landscapes*, Architectural Press, Oxford.

About the author

Émilie Pinard is a PhD candidate in architecture and anthropology at Université Laval, Canada. She holds a double master's degree in architecture, as part of which she participated in the Habitats et cultures group of Université Laval's School of Architecture. She has contributed to the development of renovation guidelines for homes of the Innu community in Uashat mak Mani-Utenam, Canada, and conducted an evaluation of a participative project run by a Canadian–Senegalese team in Malika, Senegal. Her current research concerns local practices that promote the production of housing, individual- and family-based residential strategies, and the transformation of gender relations in the urbanization of the suburbs of Dakar, Senegal.

Chapter 4

Healthy, sustainable, and culturally appropriate living and working environments: Domestic pig production in Malika, Senegal

Jessica Gagnon

Abstract

In Senegal, domestic livestock production is a means of subsistence for many house-holds. However, this practice also entails many health and environmental risks, espe-cially in cities, where these risks are exacerbated by population density, non-existent or inadequate sanitation systems, and unsuitable facilities. Urban domestic livestock facilities are often used for multiple purposes and are constrained by the competi-tion for space and restricted financial means. Moreover, breeders are rarely formally trained and are poorly equipped to respond to these risks. This study examines the breeding of pigs in a peri-urban department of Dakar and identifies and implements small-scale improvements. Using a participatory and interdisciplinary method, the study applies and considers the know-how, hopes, and beliefs of the breeders as well as the knowledge of local builders and of veterinary researchers.

Introduction

In the urban centres of Senegal, as in those of most of Africa, domestic live-stock production is a cultural practice and a subsistence strategy adopted by many households. For example, it is not uncommon to see herds of cattle and goats being driven through the streets, hen houses set up along the walls of residential buildings, or sheep being raised on rooftops right in the heart of a city (Fall and Fall, 2001; Diao, 2004). Urban livestock production thus plays an important role for many households in their daily struggle with food insecurity and poverty (Fall and Fall, 2001; Broutin et al., 2005), which are on the rise along with the acceleration of urbanization, the subsequent loss of agricultural land, the lack of local production of staple foods, and the food crisis.

Urban livestock production does have the advantage over rural livestock production in that it benefits from a greater proximity to markets for buying supplies and selling products. However, the drawbacks outweigh the advantages, with households practising urban livestock production generally being marginalized into living environments that are inadequate and precarious with regard to tenure and ownership matters (Mpozironiga et al., 2006). In cities, the health and environmental risks of domestic livestock production, today well known (Birley and Lock, 1999; Muchaal, 2002; Santandreu et al., 2005), are exacerbated due to population density, humans living in close proximity to animals, and the mix of activities that takes place in urban settings (Aboh et al., 2001; Mpozironiga et al., 2006; Rischkowsky et al., 2006; Schiere et al., 2006).

The key questions that arise are thus the following: Under what conditions is urban livestock production acceptable? And, how can the interrelation between livestock production and the urban milieu be managed so that it is safe for the environment and the people? This study aims to address these questions by examining cases of domestic pig production in Dakar suburbs.

Context and pertinence

This study is particularly interested in the concrete improvement of the environmental and sanitary conditions of domestic livestock production in the urban context. It follows in the wake of a major ecosystemic study led by a multi-disciplinary team from Senegal on the impacts of the public landfill of Greater Dakar in Malika,[1] one aspect of which concerns the domestic livestock production of pigs in Malika. Documenting environmental contamination, human and animal health, and the sanitary quality of food production, the study paints a rather bleak portrait of the conditions of living and of running smallholder pig farms in that area.

Livestock production of pigs in Malika was originally started by a small community, mainly the Manjak, who congregated and settled in what later became the Santhiaba neighbourhood. Given urbanization and its concurrent densification, pig farms there are set up in any space that is available, for example, un-serviced lots (rented by the breeders), compound courtyards, and rooms in houses under construction. There are some 80 operations of about 16 pigs each in a neighbourhood of less than 0.1 km^2.

The risks posed by this type of high-density livestock production in such close proximity to human dwellings are compounded by the associated strong environmental pollution. The soil is contaminated with faecal coliforms and, at the surface, with parasites. The well water of Malika is contaminated with microbes and excessive concentrations of suspended solids and organic matter and, in some cases, with nitrates, nitrogenous materials, and heavy metals such as lead, cadmium, and aluminium. In addition to this local contamination, heavy metals in the landfill also impact the health of the neighbourhood, by way of food scraps recuperated from the landfill by the breeders to feed their pigs (Niang et al., 2008). Figure 4.1 illustrates the presence of contaminants in domestic pig production of Santhiaba.

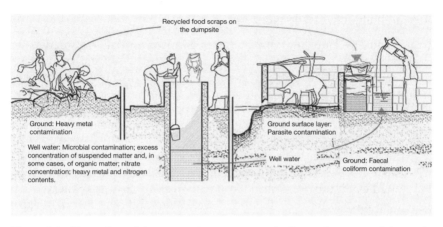

Recycled food scraps on the dumpsite

Ground: Heavy metal contamination

Well water: Microbial contamination; excess concentration of suspended matter and, in some cases, of organic matter; nitrate concentration; heavy metal and nitrogen contents.

Ground surface layer: Parasite contamination

Well water

Ground: Faecal coliform contamination

Figure 4.1 Illustration of the contaminants present in the environment of domestic livestock production

These different forms of environmental contamination impact the milieu in more ways than one. The fact that 67 per cent of pork meat produced from this community is contaminated with thermotolerant coliforms and mesophilic aerobic flora is most likely attributable to water and soil pollution as well as poor slaughter practices (Missohou, 2008).

People and animals alike are affected. The porcine livestock is mainly threatened by African swine cholera, an endemic disease in the region that is exacerbated by the shallow burying of carcasses or their disposal in landfill, as well as by the bleeding of sick animals. Missohou (2008) reports on diseases such as parasitosis, sarcoptic mange, and colibacillosis, all three of which are transmissible from pigs to humans and often related to poor maintenance conditions of pigs. The human population surveyed in Malika also suffers from parasitosis, dermatosis, buccodental infections, and respiratory diseases, the last of which are, based on a comparative analysis with other zones, probably impacted by the landfill (Tal-Dia, 2007).

Despite these risks, it would be impossible to prohibit urban livestock production. Although these different forms of contamination threaten the health of households, livestock production nevertheless has a central place in the life of the neighbourhood, especially in the daily life of women, who are the main actors in the domestic milieu and in livestock breeding. Originating in rural Manjak villages, the practice of pig farming is deeply ingrained in the culture of this community. In Santhiaba, the practice represents, for many, a tradition of sacrificial rites and animist beliefs, while others engage in it as a source of income to alleviate poverty and protect against unexpected events. This study postulates that it is possible to improve the architectural design of pig farm facilities so as to better adapt them to the urban milieu.

Research objectives and questions

Health and environmental problems related to urban livestock production depend as much on the management and the structure of the urban space (human population density in close proximity to livestock productions, collection and management of urban waste, spatial division of tasks, tenure and property management, etc.) as on the population's culture and practices of daily life and livestock production. Planning and implementing a successful intervention is thus no simple task.

The management of urban space, similar to support for livestock production, is the responsibility of the federal government and the municipalities. Many studies on urban livestock production call for a greater intervention from the state and for the adoption of regulations and tools for the support and management of this form of livestock production (Smith and Olaloku, 1998; Rischkowsky et al., 2006; Schiere et al., 2006). Policy papers tend to associate livestock production with small-scale farming in rural landscapes, and only recently has research begun to focus on intensive livestock production, which is more typical of urban livestock production. However, studies that build a bridge between research on health and environmental problems associated with pig farms and the daily reality of breeders are still rare (Wabacha et al., 2004; Thys et al., 2005).

Moreover, the built environment and the economic activities in Senegalese urban milieus depend largely on the informal sector, which is more influenced by the social dynamic and by popular practices than by government policies. In the absence of efficient municipal or state control of land development and urban sanitation systems, decisions concerning the facilities and practices of breeders, and of citizens as a whole, have significant repercussions.

Popular practices, as determining as they are, are nevertheless in the hands of actors who are generally poorly equipped to evaluate and act upon the overall implications of their practice. The breeders of Santhiaba, for example, experience chronic financial distress and, up to their recent participation in the IAGU study, had little awareness of the contamination of their milieu or of the state of health of their people and their livestock. Moreover, not being organized, they had no means to become recognized by the state in order to benefit from support or consultation services. This is compounded by the fast pace at with which peri-urban milieus, in general, are undergoing urban and cultural changes.

In recognition of this double challenge, this study aims to: 1) improve the knowledge of the contamination dynamic resulting from the interaction between people, their living environment, and livestock production, including the contaminants transmitted by livestock production; and, 2) identify and test solutions that offer a supportive and empowering environment for breeders.

Theoretical framework

The conventional solutions to the health and environmental problems generated by pig farms, such as vaccines, drugs, and manuring techniques, are poorly suited for the context of our study. These means are often costly and require professional expertise, two resources which these disadvantaged populations do not have (Pearson and Krecek, 2006; Foeken and Owuor, 2008). Even when the state or NGOs intervene to minimize these economic and technical obstacles, their effectiveness is often compromised when the measures clash with the practices and cultural values of the populations or their incapacity to understand and assimilate the guidelines and instructions provided (Pretty, 2008).

The problems of pollution, disease, and contamination cannot be approached from an exclusively technical angle. Rather, they must be studied in the context of the complex dynamic of the systems or ecosystems to which they belong. This involves studying the relationships between the physical environment, the human population, and the pig farms in order to understand the transmission of contaminants, while taking account of the economic, social, and cultural factors that influence these interactions. This constitutes the eco-health approach developed in particular by the team of Waltner-Toews et al. (2008). To arrive at a comprehensive understanding of the problems, the eco-health approach proposes a trans-disciplinary participatory method, integrating the knowledge, experience, and concerns of researchers from different disciplines, of the population affected, and of the local decision-makers. This approach, also applied by the IAGU when researching and managing projects on the impacts of the Mbeubeuss landfill, brings together representatives of the population, a group of local decision-makers, and research teams studying human health, animal health, horticulture, and the environment (e.g. air, water, soil, and waste). When identifying the ecosystemic dynamic unique to domestic pig production, our study benefited from the economic, social, health, and environmental knowledge and experience developed through this framework on the ecosystems at the periphery of the public landfill.

Complementing that comprehensive overview, this study also examines the domestic scale in more detail. In so doing, it shifts the emphasis of the study of pollution and contamination mechanisms onto the actors, in this case the breeders and the citizens, and on their involvement in shaping the architectural design of pig farm facilities. For this, the study draws on two other theoretical frameworks, namely, behavioural ecology (Moser and Weiss, 2003) and participatory ergonomics (Daniellou, 1997; Darses and Montmollin, 2006).

According to these approaches, human milieus are shaped by the culture, hopes, and constraints of the people and societies who build them. In turn, the milieus are also bearers of meanings that influence the way in which people perceive them and how they behave in them, or how they think they should behave in them. Moreover, and this is where the contribution of ergonomics comes in, the spatial configuration of a milieu influences the behaviour, composure, and repertoire of movements and actions that people adopt. Milieus and people thus influence each other at the spatial as well as cultural level. The identification of the dynamic interactions of this interrelation between people their milieus constitutes the particular contribution of this project to other works in progress on Malika. Figure 4.2 presents an illustration that integrates the three theoretical frameworks on which this study is founded.

Approach and results

With the aim of documenting and improving the development and practices of livestock production, the adopted approach was that of research and action, a process realized in two large phases aiming to: 1) identify the problems; and then, 2) formulate, test (on site), and evaluate solutions. Inspired by the WIND (Work Improvement in Neighbourhood Development) approach (Kogi, 2006; Kawakami, 2008) of the ILO, this process of identifying small improvements was integrated into a broader concept that drew on local 'good examples' and that involved the collaboration of the breeders, one researcher and one student in veterinary science (both IAGU affiliated), and me, a young researcher in architecture.

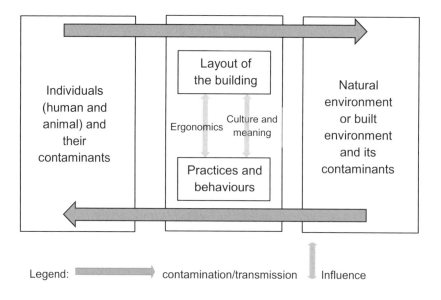

Figure 4.2 Illustration showing the integration of the three theoretical research frameworks

Explorations of the practices and the milieu of livestock production

The approach

The research phase, aiming to explore the biosecurity of the domestic dynamics and the practices of livestock production in Santhiaba, was realized through exchanges with the breeders. Established by taking account of the experiences of a veterinarian and the knowledge gathered in a review of the literature on the health and environmental impacts of diverse forms of development of livestock production, a questionnaire and an observation method were developed with the view to researching in a participatory manner. These activities allowed the breeders to be identified and, through them, develop an understanding of their practices, their milieus, and the interactions between them and their milieus. These research methods were complemented by architectural and photographic measurement drawings. As a whole, this approach allowed for the characterization of the architecture of the milieus, the practices of livestock production, and the transmission dynamic of the contaminants and pollutants.

The results

These investigations shed light on certain shortcomings of the practices and equipment used in livestock production. One of the main problems identified concerns the surroundings of the pig farms, which are generally used for both livestock production and domestic and public purposes. The impact of livestock production activities reaches beyond the walls of the pig farm: during the rainy season, the liquid pig manure runs off down holes dug in the streets used by residents of the neighbourhood and by roaming dogs, goats, and poultry. Moreover, the front sections of the pens serve as a storage place for barrels of food, tools (for food maintenance and preparation), and old tools and equipment. It is also the place where the breeders perform some of the livestock production tasks and a space where people stop when transferring between the pig farm and the domestic milieu. In most cases, this space also overlaps with that of a courtyard in which multiple domestic activities take place, such as clothes drying, children's play, rest, socializing, and the roaming of sheep and dogs. This cohabitation bears risks of a transfer of contaminants and is exacerbated by the lack of certain practices, for example, stored tools are often only rinsed and breeders neither change nor disinfect their shoes before entering or leaving the pen or before going from one pen to another.

The considerable height of the entry gates of the pig farms, on average 0.9 m from the ground, is also problematic. Although sometimes compensated by improvised steps or landings, blocks of piled up concrete, or turned-over buckets or basins, the height of the entry gates generally makes it difficult for older breeders to enter and leave the pen, which has repercussions for the maintenance of the pen. It also has an impact on the transfer of the pigs to slaughter or the isolation of sows for parturition. These activities can only be done with the assistance of neighbours or relatives, who, by moving within the milieus of livestock production, then become vectors of the transmission and dissemination of pathogens.

The roofs, made of a mix of recuperated materials (e.g. cloth, fabric, and zinc sheets), cover only a small portion of the pen area and are not sealed tight. They thus offer the pigs only weak protection against the sun and adverse weather conditions, which increases the level of stress among the animals, subsequently decreasing their appetite (heat effect) and productivity. Moreover, the accumulation of rainwater in the pens provokes the drowning of piglets, which, once intermixed with the liquid pig manure, increases the quantity of waste to manage.

As the floors of the pens are very rarely tiled, the accumulation of water promotes the percolation of the liquid pig manure, contaminating the water table, which is very high in this area. As this water serves as drinking water for the human population and for the pigs, its contamination has health effects and promotes the spreading of diseases. Moreover, the soil becomes clayish and slippery by being mixed with liquid pig manure, which causes falls and thereby injuries. During the dry season, the pollutants and contaminants in this liquid pig manure are furthermore spread when the liquid pig manure is swept up and deposited on the outskirts of the neighbourhood, in a zone where goats roam and eat and where children play soccer. In the rainy season, the holes down which the liquid pig manure is drained function as veritable funnels that amplify the percolation of liquid pig manure.

The surfaces of the walls, usually made of concrete blocks and sometimes of recuperated materials (e.g. zinc sheets, PVC pipes, or fibre cement), are difficult to clean and, as a result, trap contaminants and parasites. The zinc sheets used to build the pig farms, similar to the zinc barrels used to store food scraps and drinking water for the pigs, rust with time and develop cutting edges. The breeders, aware of this risk of injury, thus try to limit the handling of the barrels, which explains why the barrels are often not washed before being filled up with new food scraps.

Once identified, the problems concerning the architectural set-up and the practices of livestock production were validated and identified by means of an interdisciplinary experimental phase. The goal was to evaluate the health and environmental impacts with regard to different shortcomings identified by various disciplines, to explore improvement solutions, and to prioritize areas for improvement. The approach consisted of exploring architectural improvements to existing facilities by holding two roundtables composed of Quebec experts and researchers, and a third roundtable held in Dakar comprising members and researchers of the IAGU. This yielded a number of recommended intervention measures for the pig farms, which concerned namely: 1) the roofs and the management of the surrounding conditions; 2) floor coverings and the management of the liquid pig manure; 3) the entry gate and work ergonomics; and 4) the distinction between the livestock production facility and the domestic space, and preventative measures.

Development of ideas to improve the pig farms

The approach

Because the improvement of the pig farms was part of a larger intervention project of the IAGU for the entire community of breeders, the second research phase took place in direct collaboration with the IAGU programme. In a sense, this phase became the pilot phase for future interventions concerning all domestic pig farm owners of the neighbourhood[2] and the first step of a neighbourhood development process. It began with a long period of consultation and harmonization in order to arrive, together with the neighbourhood and the diverse stakeholders, at a collective vision and a shared approach. For the purposes of this study, this involved planning and decision-making with the pre-existing consultation team, composed of representatives of an economic interest group that already existed in the neighbourhood and which the representatives of the breeders joined in the framework of the project.[3]

The participatory design process began with an activity involving all the breeders who own their livestock productions and during which a design group was set up and mandated to devise possible improvements. This group, which represented the bridge from and to the community, was composed of volunteers, among them six breeders from the domestic milieu and three breeders working in construction. The veterinary student participating in the project, a neighbourhood businessman, and a community facilitator also played an active role in this group. The participatory design activities concerned each of the big four areas of improvement identified with the Senegalese experts. The discussions, aiming to encourage the identification of simple, inexpensive, and ergonomically and culturally adapted solutions, were based on photos of the different types of developments identified in the neighbourhood and focused on developing good development criteria. At this occasion, breeders and technical consultants were also able to share their knowledge and visions. In a second step, the results of these meetings were the object of discussions and validations of the IAGU-affiliated researchers as well as the builders and architects. In a concluding step, the results were presented and explained by the members of the participatory design group to all those benefiting from the improvements.

The results

The participatory design workshops identified four priority tasks. The first comprised the addition of a low wall separating the pen from the rest of the compound, in order to delimit the space for materials storage and livestock production. This separation was also intended to serve as the opportunity to implement new practices, namely, the changing of shoes and clothing when changing between the area of livestock production and the domestic milieu, and the restriction of access to the pig farm to anyone who is not a breeder. The second task involved the lowering of the entry gates to 0.6 m from the ground, to prevent the piglets from running away and to facilitate access to the pen by the breeders. This measure was also intended to allow the breeders to move the pigs out of the pens on their own. Full metal doors were added to block the opening and to limit the view into the interior of the pen. The third task comprised the addition of new roofs and support columns, covering the entire pen area, in order to limit the entry of water in the pig farms. For this, one section of the roof was covered with translucent materials, permitting the entry of solar rays, in turn allowing for a certain degree of drying and sanitization of the liquid pig manure. A second section of the roof, made of metal sheets, provided a shaded area. This set-up, comprising two different zones in the pen, was designed to reinforce the natural inclination of the pigs to use one part, the more comfortable part, of the pen for rest and the second part for urination and defecation. Task number four consisted of removing the dirty floor of the pens and of building a concrete slab, a drainage system, and a ditch allowing for liquid pig manure to be contained and collected so that it could then be sent to the composting facilities.

Experimentation with and adaptation of the general improvements

The approach

The improvement was planned for 4 of the 16 pig farms, with the remaining improvements to be realized in three other phases by the IAGU. To improve the understanding and capacity of the breeders to intervene in their milieu of livestock production, the breeders formed four groups based on the resemblance of the set-up of their pig farms and their integration with the surrounding compounds. Each group included at minimum one breeder who participated in the design, so as to allow each group to benefit from the particular expertise of these breeders and to strengthen the capacity of the participating breeders to transmit their knowledge. Discussion workshops held in the compounds by the volunteers shed light on ways of choosing and adjusting the improvement proposals on the basis of the particular type of production set-up.

The subsequent construction phase then allowed for the fine-tuning of the proposed improvements, this time on the basis of the construction methods and local competencies. Benefiting from the presence of workers within the neighbourhood, and in the spirit of strengthening the local capacities in construction, nearly all workers were selected from the community, among them members from the participatory design team and sons of breeders. I managed the construction sites in collaboration with a Quebec architectural intern and a supervisor of the Dakar construction site as well as in ongoing consultation with the breeders concerned and sometimes their families. This mix of actors offered a framework suitable for an exchange of viewpoints and experiences and for the continual adjustment of the planned improvements.

The results

The exchanges during these adjustment phases not only allowed the improvement of the planned changes but also, and above all, the anticipation of the constraints facing the works. The roof, for which no local 'good example' existed, was the most difficult improvement to adapt economically, culturally, and technically. The raising of the roof, necessary for good ventilation of the pen and good accessibility for the breeders, had the drawback of allowing outsiders to look inside the pen when the pen lined the street. Thus, responding to the breeders' stated need for discretion in their operations, the plan was to raise the wall with Claustra blocks. Building the roof was also a challenge, namely because it had many joints and required a high and relatively costly level of precision. More generally, building a roof requires striking a balance between cost and durability. Given the limited financial means of the breeders, the modest construction of their houses, and the speed of the changes taking place in the domestic milieu and peri-urban neighbourhoods, sustainable constructions could prove inappropriate. Lastly, the building methods generally depend on the experience and technical knowledge of the workers. Most of the workers involved in the project had neither training nor experience in construction. Building in such a context is thus largely based on learning by doing and the sharing of experience between workers.

The adaptation phases of the general improvements and the construction phase placed emphasis above all on the people involved in the participatory design and their understanding and vision of the improvements. Based on the exchanges taking place during the project, the desired appropriation of the process was very different from one actor to the next. One part of them appropriated certain notions shared by the researchers to the point of promoting them, while the older women of the group were not in a position to present the developed improvements to the other woman breeders. This disparity can be attributable to different factors. The older women were, as was identified later, not fully in command of the Wolof language that was used for all activities. Moreover, even though the improvements were supposed to be achieved with readily available, everyday means, the design did include certain construction concepts that were unknown to some of the actors. Some concepts related to contamination dynamics were also difficult to reconcile with the belief system of the Manjak culture, which considers disease and mortality to result from occult forces rather than from scientifically verifiable facts.

Nevertheless, the voluntary involvement of the members of the participatory design group to support the other breeders and the workers in the three construction phases, along with the evolution of skills and knowledge ensuring the succession of phases, demonstrate a good level of appropriation of the project. This pursuit of activities over time will allow for the dissemination of new ways of building pig farms and for the development of renewed understandings of the dynamic of contaminant spreading. The realized constructions also constitute models for a revision of building methods in livestock production.

Research follow-up

Considering the variable assimilation of knowledge during the research activities, further efforts should be made to strengthen the breeders' knowledge. Veterinary check-ups and training on health practices and preventative measures, to be conducted by the IAGU with the breeders, will respond to that need. The same applies to the support given to the breeders' association, which, provided for one year starting at end of August 2010 by an IAGU-affiliated expert, should strengthen the connections made in 2009 during the neighbourhood interventions. Lastly, the Habitats et cultures team of Université Laval is planning to undertake periodic evaluations over the two next years of the performance of the new constructions and their usage, as well as the perceptions and practices of the breeders, the workers, and the inhabitants of the neighbourhood.

Discussion and lessons learned

The results of the research portion of this project complement existing knowledge on the developments and practices of livestock production in the urban and domestic milieu by highlighting the importance of considering not only the area used directly for livestock production but also the larger compound. The results also show that a process linking the daily practices, beliefs, knowledge, expertise, and building practices of the breeders with the expertise of researchers and specialists, although possibly time-consuming and demanding, allows for the development of livestock production practices that are appropriate and above all accepted by all stakeholders. The breeders are first-tier actors in the evolution of the health and environmental conditions of the urban milieu. Public servants and experts should therefore take the time to listen to breeders and work with them on the development of new practices and technologies. Moreover, state interventions in domestic livestock production should emphasize the on-site transfer of technologies and interventions taking place within this context.

Future studies

The developed solutions, although founded on proven principles of building healthy facilities, should be evaluated to measure their real impact on the improvement of health and environmental conditions in domestic operations. A quantitative and qualitative evaluation would allow for the establishment of the cost–benefit ratio of these improvements, in addition to convincing decision-makers and experts of the advantages of promoting their replication.

Further research should also be pursued in architecture to develop improvements that are respectful of the financial and technical means of the breeders.

Acknowledgements

This project is a collective work and results from the active and generous participation of many stakeholders who I cannot thank enough. Thank you, first of all, to the professors who gave me advice and support: Denise Piché and André Casault, professors at the School of Architecture of Université Laval, and Louise Lachapelle, teacher at Collège Maisonneuve and researcher. I also thank the members and affiliated researchers of the IAGU, among them Oumar Cissé, director; Ayao Missohou, professor and researcher at the École Inter-États des Sciences et Médecine Vétérinaires de Dakar (EISMV); Évariste Bassène, veterinarian; and Ms Fatou Diop, community facilitator, for their work, continuous involvement, support, and invaluable advice.

I furthermore wish to extend my thanks to all the people with whom I had the privilege of working on a daily basis: Gontran Mendy and Isidore Gomis (translators and advisors), Antoine Gomis (neighbourhood representative who invested a lot of time to bring together and inform the breeders and to become their spokesperson), and Véronique Preira, Rose Gomis, Rose Coréa, Thérèse Diatta, Antoinette Diatta, Peter Mendy, Laurent Mendy, François Gomis, Christophe Apolinaire Mendy, and Charles Ambass (members of the participatory design group) for their dedicated participation in the development of the improvements and the awareness-raising work among the breeders of the neighbourhood. I also thank all breeders from Santhiaba for their warm welcome and their participation, as well as the workers, Alain Filiatrault (architectural intern), and Ibrahima Faye (construction site foreman) for their dedicated contribution to realizing the improvements and for the rewarding exchanges. Thank you also to Mouhamadou Naby Kane (architect and director of the Collège Universitaire d'Architecture de Dakar) for his valuable advice and generous availability.

In addition I thank the following people for their valuable contribution to the round-table activities: Stéphane Godbout (researcher at the IRDA), Sylvain Pigeon (project manager at BPR), Frédéric Guay (professor at the department of animal sciences of Université Laval), Hélène Trépanier and Anne Leboeuf (from the Institut national de santé animale of Quebec's Ministère de l'Agriculture, des Pêcheries et de l'Alimentation), F. Carl Uhland (student in veterinary medicine at the Université de Montréal), Marc Trudelle (agroenvironmental consultant for the Fédération des producteurs de porcs du Quebec), Nick Bachand (Master's candidate in veterinary sciences, option epidemiology), Martine Denicourt (visiting professor at the department of clinical sciences of the Université de Montréal), Josée Harel (professor at the department of pathology and microbiology of the Université de Montréal), and Cheikh Fall (professor and researcher at the Institut de Santé et Développement de Dakar).

Finally, I thank IDRC for having funded and supported this project.

Notes

1 These are two research projects coordinated by the IAGU: 'Impacts et amélioration dans conditions de vie et de l'environnement à Diamalaye', a project financed in the framework of the urban poverty and environment programme UPE of IDRC; and 'Site d'enfouissement de Mbeubeuss: Étude de l'impact sur la santé humaine à Diamalaye (Malika) utilisant une approche écosanté (Sénégal)', a project financed in the framework of the Ecohealth programme of IDRC.
2 The pilot project of the IAGU also included building a community pig farm in a rural zone for operators who would rent the pig farm. The planning of this pig farm, conducted together with the neighbourhood bodies, took place concurrently to this research phase.
3 It would go beyond the scope of this article to describe all the stages of the decision-making process. However, all intervention stages here presented were discussed and decided on with this advisory body, which is also where it was determined that the interventions in the domestic pig farms would target owners only and that the renting breeders were to be gradually moved to the community pig farm, and that the first interventions would be done with a sub-group of four or five breeders.

References

Aboh, A. B., Ouedraogo, S., Rivera, A. M., Pham Ti, H. H., and Mekhtoub, K. (2001) 'Importance, contraintes et voies de développement des élevages urbains et périurbains dans la région sud-Bénin', Working development series, International Centre for development oriented Research in Agriculture (ICRA), Montpelier.

Birley, M. H. and Lock, K. (eds) (1999) *The Health Impacts of Peri-urban Natural Resource Development*, International Centre for Health Impact Assessment Liverpool School of Tropical Medicine, University of Liverpool, Liverpool.

Broutin, C., Floquet, A., Seck, P., Tossou, R., and Edja, H. (2005) 'Agriculture et élevage face aux contraintes et opportunités de l'expansion urbaine: Exploration autour des villes de Thiès et Mboro au Sénégal et d'Abomey-Bohicon et Para-kou au Bénin', Presentation at the workshop Agricultures et développement urbain en Afrique centrale et de l'Ouest, Centre de coopération internationale en recherche agronomique pour le développement (Cirad)/Ministère des Affaires Étrangères et Européennes (MAE), Yaoundé.

Daniellou, F. (1997) *Comprendre le travail pour le transformer, la pratique de l'ergonomie*, ANACT, Toulouse.

Darses, F. and Montmollin, M. D. (2006) *L'ergonomie*, La Découverte, Paris.

Diao, M. B. (2004) 'Situation et contraintes des systèmes urbains et périurbains de production horticole et animale dans la région de Dakar', *Cahiers Agricultures* 13(1): 39–49.

Fall, S. T. and Fall, A. S. (2001) 'Conclusion générale: Quelle agriculture urbaine pour le Sénégal ?', in S. T. Fall and A. S. Fall (eds) *Cités horticoles en sursis? L'agriculture urbaine dans les grandes Niayes au Sénégal*, pp. 117–26, International Development Research Centre (IDRC), Ottawa.

Foeken, D. W. J. and Owuor, S. O. (2008) 'Farming as a livelihood source for the urban poor of Nakuru, Kenya', *Geoforum* 39(6): 1978–90.

Kawakami, T., Van, V. N., Theu, V. N., Khai T. T., and Kogi K. (2008) 'Participatory support to farmers in improving safety and health at work: Building WIND farmer volunteer networks in Viet Nam', *Industrial Health* 46: 455–62.

Kogi, K. (2006) 'Advances in participatory occupational health aimed at good practices in small enterprises and the informal sector', *Health* 44: 31–4.

Ly, C. and Duteurtre, G. (eds) (2005) 'Pour des politiques d'élevage "partagées" – Actes de l'Atelier Regional sur les Politiques d'Élevage – Dakar 17 et 18 novembre 2004', FAO Initiative pour des politiques d'élevagee en faveur des pauvres, ISRA, CIRAD, DIREL, ODVS, PLPPI Meeting report, www.fao. org/ag/againfo/programmes/en/pplpi/docarc/mrp_partagees.pdf

Missohou, A. (2008) *Typologie, productivité et qualité des produits animaux en aviculture et en porciculture autour de la décharge de Mbeubeuss à Malika au Sénégal*, Service de Zootechnie-Alimentation, École Inter-États des Sciences et Médecine Vétérinaires, Dakar.

Moser, G. and Weiss, K. (2003) *Espaces de vie: aspects de la relation homme-environnement*, A. Colin, Paris.

Mpozironiga, A., Broutin, C., Gueye, M., and Sokona, K. (2006) 'La filière avicole de ponte à Thiès-Fandène, dynamique et devenir face à l'expansion urbaine', Document de travail Écocité 14, Gret, Enda Graf, Dakar.

Muchaal, P. K. (2002) *Urban Agriculture and Zoonoses in West Africa: An Assessment of the Potential Impact on Public Health Part A: Literature Review*, International Development Research Centre (IDRC), Ottawa.

Niang, S., Sarr, B., Pfeifer, H.-R., Gueye-Girardet, A., Gaye, M. L., Ndiaye, M. L., et al. (2008) 'La décharge de Mbeubeuss Impact sur les ressources en eau et le sol', Provisional final report. Laboratoire de traitement des eaux usées, Université Cheikh Anta Diop, Dakar.

Pearson, R. A. and Krecek, R. C. (2006) 'Delivery of health and husbandry improvements to working animals in Africa', *Tropical Animal Health and Production* 38: 93–101.

Pretty, J. (2008) 'Agricultural sustainability: Concepts, principles and evidence', *Philosophical Transactions of the Royal Society B-Biological Sciences* 363(1491): 447–65.

Rischkowsky, B., Siegmund-Schultze, M., Bednarz, K., and Killanga, S. (2006) 'Urban sheep keeping in West Africa: Can socioeconomic household profiles explain management and productivity?', *Human Ecology* 34(6): 785–807.

Santandreu, A., Castro, G., and Ronca, F. (2005) 'Urban pig farming in irregular settlements in Uruguay', *Urban Agriculture Magazine* 1(2), www.ruaf. org/node/129 [accessed 5 January 2011].

Schiere, H., Thys, E., Matthys, F., and Rischkowsky, B. (2006) 'Livestock keeping in urbanised areas', in R. van Veenhuizen (ed.) *Cities Farming for the Future: Urban Agriculture for Green and Productive Cities*, pp. 350–79, RUAF Foundation, IDRC, and IIRR, Ottawa.

Smith, O. B. and Olaloku, E. A. (1998) *Peri-Urban Livestock Production Systems*, Cities Feeding People Series, Report 24, International Development Research Centre (IDRC), Ottawa.

Tal-Dia, A. (2007) 'Preliminary report of the article Décharge de Mbeubeuss: Analyse des impacts et amélioration des conditions de vie des populations de Diamalaye à Malika dans la banlieue de Dakar (Sénégal)', Institut de Santé et de Développement (ISED), Institut Africain de Gestion Urbaine (IAGU), Dakar.

Thys, E., Oueadraogo, M., Speybroeck, N., and Geerts, S. (2005) 'Socio-economic determinants of urban household livestock keeping in semi-arid Western Africa', *Journal of Arid Environments* 63(2): 475–96.

Wabacha, J. K., Maribei, J. M., Mulei, C. M., Kyule, M. N., Zessin, K. H., and Oluoch-Kosura, W. (2004) 'Characterisation of smallholder pig production in Kikuyu Division, central Kenya', *Preventive Veterinary Medicine* 63: 183–95.

Waltner-Toews, D., Kay, J.J., and Lister, N. "The Ecosystem Approach: Complexity, Uncertainty, and Managing for Sustainability" for the Columbia University press series: *Complexity in Ecological Systems*. New York: Columbia University Press, 2008.

About the author

Jessica Gagnon holds a professional master's degree in architecture from Université Laval, Quebec City, Canada, where she is currently completing a research master's degree in architectural science. Her professional and research interests focus on the interactions between people and the built environment as well as on participatory methods for sharing knowledge between dwellers and professionals from varied disciplines. Through her research work in Senegal, she specialized in both domestic and construction ergonomics.

Chapter 5

Housing for the urban poor through informal providers, Dhaka, Bangladesh

Mohamed Kamruzzaman

Abstract

Dhaka is experiencing a severe housing crisis. This especially affects the urban poor, most of whom build their own dwellings through private or community efforts, referred to as self-help or piecemeal housing production. This study looks at the current shelter supply practices and strategies of these informal providers and examines their ability to provide decent housing. For this, it conducted a survey of the activities of informal builders in a typical residential area of Dhaka, covering 1,089 housing plots. The study also included an ethnographic observation, a survey questionnaire, and longitudinal fieldwork. Further aspects that were taken into consideration are the crucial role of owner-builders, landlords, and small-scale builders in providing shelter for the vast influx of tenants in the city, as well as in meeting Dhaka's physical expansion needs, planning visions, and consolidation strategies.

Introduction

The need to scale up housing production in the Global South through all possible means has now been acknowledged by all policy-makers and commentators in this field (Okpala, 1992; World Bank, 1993; Tipple, 1994; UNCHS, 1996). However, in most cities of the Global South, including Dhaka, Bangladesh, the strategies for providing public housing have failed to meet the needs of the urban poor.

In the cities and villages of Bangladesh, housing is produced through private or community efforts, referred to as self-help or piecemeal housing production. The resulting developments, combining contemporary technology with traditional techniques and designs, range from being bland and monotonous to inchoate and eclectic. Nevertheless, as such housing does meet practical needs, the contributions of piecemeal developers should not be ignored, in particular with the view to improving policy-making. Yet, the handful of studies that exist on self-help and piecemeal housing are mainly descriptive and do not provide an adequate understanding of the production strategies.

This study comprises an investigation of how informal builders in the cities and villages of Bangladesh are capable of producing shelters in light of the difficulties they face, uses their housing construction techniques as a case study, and examines their potential for improvement. Through a combination of ethnographic observation, a survey questionnaire, and longitudinal fieldwork, the study highlights the crucial role of owner-builders, landlords, and small-scale builders in providing shelter for the vast influx of tenants in the city.

Objective of the study

Urban housing demand in Dhaka has essentially been fulfilled by the private sector, generally comprised of self-help owner-builders, small-scale builders, and their associates. This sector provides ready-to-occupy housing units for rent for the vast majority of middle- and lower-middle-income population. The first question addressed by this study is: How does the local population manage to construct modern houses in the absence of technical know-how, formal financing, and construction experience? This chapter focuses on construction processes and aims to:

- identify the self-help housing activities in the study area;
- explore the process of building modern apartments by piecemeal construction;
- determine the extent to which self-help piecemeal housing construction is practised in the city's housing market.

In so doing, it seeks to identify the unique operational strategies of informal builders and how these contribute to scaling up housing production.

Research methodology

Four neighbourhood areas of the Rupnagar Residential Area (RRA) in Mirpur, Dhaka, were selected for investigation in order to identify characteristic features of physical expansion in self-help housing[1] developments. The selection of these study areas was guided by three principles: 1) the area had to be representative; 2) the area had to be newly developed and include culturally rooted housing construction styles; and 3) the area had to include popular contemporary housing types. The characteristics of the selected RRA neighbourhood areas meet these three major criteria and allowed us to better understand the prevalent housing construction scenario in the study area.

The study is based primarily on data from interviews with 50 owner-builders, census materials, and ethnographic observations of 1,089 housing plots. The 50 owner-builders were selected randomly from four neighbouring areas in the RRA. A questionnaire consisting of 135 structured questions was directed at household heads, i.e. owner-builders or their representatives. Physical observations of all housing plots in the study area were undertaken in order to determine housing types, construction types, building materials, providers, building height, number of dwelling units, as well as development length.

Context of self-help housing in Bangladesh

Bangladesh is a predominantly rural country, where self-help building still plays a significant role in traditional peasant communities. Rural housing in Bangladesh has been largely based on the use of locally available resources as prime building materials in a process of self-help building undertaken by the community. This type of building is thus suitable for environments with widely available natural resources and encourages people's direct involvement in the building process. In the past, local availability of natural building materials and their employment in self-help construction sustained traditional architecture. However, in recent decades, traditional self-help building processes have been greatly affected if not changed entirely due to the advent of the cash economy, industrialization, scarcity of natural resources, and population pressure. In Bangladesh, affluent households are increasingly shifting to manufactured materials and to hiring skilled builders, while middle- and lower-middle-income households still turn to self-help piecemeal construction as a viable option.

Construction materials

Bamboo and thatching materials are two main natural building materials. The results of a national survey in 1982 showed that more than 60 per cent of all households in Bangladesh lived in houses that used bamboo as a main building material, and less than 5 per cent of houses were built of manufactured materials such as brick and cement (BBS, 1988). However, these natural materials are gradually becoming expensive and less readily available. The use of bricks for walls and corrugated iron sheets for roofs is more prevalent in urban areas and is affordable by the majority of affluent households. In the recent past, people have become more accustomed to using bricks, cement, sand, and steel, despite their high cost. At the same time, the use of traditional building materials has been rapidly declining due to changes in lifestyle, dwelling habits, and trends towards Western-style living in the urban areas in Bangladesh, including Dhaka City. The provision of housing is thus highly dependent on the availability of building materials, and the cost of housing has gone up due to increased construction activities, the use of high-cost building materials and components, and inadequate building supplies.

Urban housing through self-help construction

Self-help is characteristic of most traditional housing. This does not necessarily imply that a household possesses all the skills to build a house on its own.

Quite often, the services of specialist builders are required, who usually do not receive payment in the form of cash but in exchange for food or future favours from the household. The specialist might be a family friend or neighbour, and his role and service is a commonplace feature of the community. As most members of the community are in command of basic construction skills, help from the specialist is required only for specific tasks. For example, building a roof requires a specialist, while the rest of the house can be built by the household. When necessary, extra labour is also paid for in kind. Supervision of house construction is usually conducted by households that have no experience with the technical aspects of construction, and hence supervision is generally not adequate (Ahmed, 1998).

There are three common ways of building a house on a self-help basis in Dhaka: 1) complete self-help; 2) partial self-help; and 3) contract basis. In the first type, households recruit masons, carpenters, and several assistants from a nearby location and have the house built under their own supervision. In addition, family members frequently assist with the transportation of building materials and the finishing of interior walls and floors. In the second type, the household assigns the major tasks to a master masonry worker, steel workers, and carpenters, whom they pay on a per volume-of-work basis. These households also hire day labourers for smaller tasks, yet take charge of supervision. In the third type, households assign all the work to small-scale builders. Here, the homeowner only supplies the materials and supervises the construction.

Study area

We begin by outlining a few features of the study area[2] that are pertinent for understanding issues of housing development in these settlements. To alleviate the housing problem in Dhaka City, the National Housing Authority (NHA) embarked on the RRA housing project in 1982. Still under development, this project is located in the outskirts of Dhaka City, in Mirpur, about 6 km from the city centre. It spreads over 35 ha of land divided into 1,200 plots of different sizes, 31 of which were designated as commercial in order to be able to generate revenue. The project caters by and large to the middle class and has plots earmarked for schools, colleges, a park, a hospital, a lake, a shopping mall, and other public amenities. For the purposes of this study, the area was divided into four parts in order to simplify the analysis of the development pattern. Part 1 included the plots between roads 1 and 10; Part 2 those between roads 11 and 16; Part 3 those between roads 17 and 23; and Part 4 those between roads 24 and 33.

The plot sizes of these projects were examined and found to range between 117 and 335 m^2. In Part 1, all plots had an area of 335m^2, and in Part 2, 234m^2, with the exception of a few corner plots. Plots in Part 3 spanned 167m^2, and those in Part 4 117m^2. The minimum plot size was 117m^2 (in Part 4) and the maximum plot size 335m^2 (in Part 1). The typical plot was rectangular in shape and oriented along the north–south axis, with the house built along the east–west axis to avoid direct sunlight from the east and west and to capture the breeze. In the RRA, housing settlement takes the shape of a rectilinear gridiron pattern. Plots are arranged along the main road at inclines of about 10° in Part 2, 15° in Part 3, and 30° in Part 4, with respect to the north axis. The gross population density of the RRA is about 1,925 persons per hectare, and population density increases gradually from Part 1 to Part 4.

Piecemeal construction of multi-storey apartments

In piecemeal construction, the building process takes place incrementally over time. However, this does not necessarily mean that the design of the building layout and the construction stages are improvised over time. Very often, builders have the final architectural plan of their building project ready from the start, but simply stretch out the construction process over a long period of time. Homeowners generally move into semi-finished buildings and then gradually continue the construction according to choice, need, and affordability. The main reason for the prevalence of this type of construction is the lack of external financing to cover construction costs.

Construction phases of different building types

Before identifying the different construction phases, we present the different building types: 1) temporary houses; 2) semi-permanent houses; and 3) permanent houses (apartments). Most households begin by obtaining ownership of the land. For this, the households, in this case slum dwellers, build some form of temporary structure in order to secure land possession. Sometimes they pay a lump-sum rent and sometimes they stay on a freehold basis. Temporary houses are locally known as 'kutcha' houses. Kutchas generally have an earthen plinth with bamboo (sometimes timber) posts and walls and a roof made of temporary materials. The walls are made of straw, jute sticks, mud, and unburnt bricks. Roofs may be made from thatch such as rice, wheat, maize straw, or catkin grass, along with split bamboo. In the study area, the highest percentages (10 per cent) of temporary houses are found in Part 1, where the plots are large (Figure 5.1).

Semi-permanent houses are locally known as 'semi-pucca' houses. They have shallow brick foundations with brick soling and ordinary floor finishes. Walls are often built with brick or corrugated iron sheets. Roofs are made of corrugated iron sheets with timber frames or steel angle framing. Generally, the workers have no formal training, with masonry workers receiving on-the-job training from their superiors. In this type of housing, the owner functions as architect, mason, and engineer all in one. The houses are L-shaped or U-shaped with a central courtyard ensuring maximum utilization of land. A typical semi-pucca house is comprised of six to eight rental units and is very affordable. As such it is a very popular form of housing, as there is a

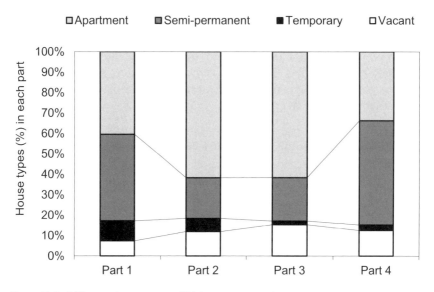

Figure 5.1 Different house types (%) in each part of the RRA

huge demand for cheap rental units in all four parts of the study area. There is not a significant difference in rental income between a semi-*pucca* house and an apartment building, although the investment cost for the latter type of housing is quite large. For this reason, households often begin by building semi-*pucca* houses and accumulate rental income, which they then invest in building apartments. This trend is confirmed by the presence of a large number of semi-*pucca* housing units in the four study areas.

Permanent houses are generally referred to as '*pucca*' houses and are usually intended to serve as apartments. The apartments in the study can be classified into two different structural forms. The first type is a load-bearing brick structure and the other a reinforced concrete frame structure. A 10 inch (25 cm) brick wall was traditionally used as the load-bearing wall in the first type and a 5 inch partition wall in the latter type. For both forms, roofs are constructed with reinforced concrete and floors with mosaic tiles according to the capabilities, preferences, and motifs of the households. Apartments made with a load-bearing brick structure are gradually disappearing because of their unsuitability for vertical expansion (less than 5 per cent are apartments). Apartments are the most preferred housing option in the study area. The highest percentage (61.7 per cent) of multi-storey apartments are in Part 3. Some 49.4 per cent of all housing plots in the RRA are developed as multi-storey apartments.

Apartment construction

The buyers of the plots, mostly from the middle class, were offered land to buy at a subsidized rate through a government site and service scheme. The cost of the land was thus less of a burden on the households than the cost of construction. The entire financing for construction costs during the various stages is provided by the households from their own savings, informal loans from relatives or friends, and the selling of assets of their rural origins. The long-term goal of the households is a monetary return on investments through the addition of rental units. Almost all the interviewed households (90 per cent) indicated wanting to invest in housing in order to ensure decent living accommodation within the city and to secure income generation, as well as a source of income for when they are older.

The households developed prototypical layouts that permit a variety of incremental transformations. The key elements ensuring this versatility are: a building system that can accommodate additions and repartitioning; and a staircase to future upper floors, conveniently located close to street level to allow for the internal partitioning of the floor area into independent units. The households thus choose multi-storey apartments built with reinforced concrete frame structures, which allow for vertical expansion and internal partitioning for future rental accommodation.

Households contract out construction to workers in the building trades. They retain control of the pace of construction, set the priorities, choose between alternatives, and decide on the sequencing of the work steps. The workers freely replicate, adapt, and blend building techniques and styles. The choice of materials and systems is dictated by cost, practicality, and expediency. The choice of motifs and colours is determined by both the builder and the tenants, who generally share a dislike of old-fashioned styles.

An illustration of the complete piecemeal construction phases[3] taking place in the surveyed plots is shown in Figure 5.2, with the exception of, for reasons of simplicity, certain micro-construction phases. Households generally set up a boundary wall (phase A) soon after purchasing and finishing the land registration process. This involves no significant construction works or experience since the process is limited to brick work. All of the interviewed households had built either a temporary or semi-permanent structure after having purchased their land. To retain possession of the land, slum dwellers often build temporary housing, which, as explained earlier, is tolerated by the landowners. In most cases, households construct semi-permanent structures (phase B), which require less capital, construction time, and construction skills – but which nevertheless generate a handsome rental income. In the surveyed plots, 42 per cent of housing structures in Part 1, 20 per cent in Part 2, 21 per cent in Part 3, and 51 per cent in Part 4 are semi-permanent housing. Semi-permanent structures in the whole study area comprise, on average, 33 per cent of all housing structures.

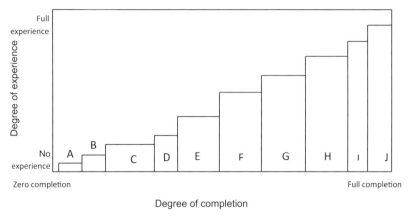

Constructions phases:

Phase A: Construction of boundary wall
Phase B: Construction of temporary/semi-permanent house
Phase C: Sub-surface construction/pile driving/sand filling
Phase D: Construction of girders, columns, and brick works
Phase E: Casting of roof slab (either partial or full)
Phase F: Finishing the ground floor (owner's portion)
Phase G: Finishing the ground floor (tenant's portion)
Phase H: Construction of staircase, columns of next floor
Phase I: Casting the roof slab of next floor (partial or full)
Phase J: Finishing the next floor (partial or full)

Figure 5.2 Typical model of piecemeal construction process

Generally, the households take some time before starting the foundation works for apartments. The goal is to accumulate the required capital for apartment construction from rental income from semi-permanent housing. In this way, semi-permanent houses are often treated as stepping stones towards the building of apartments (Photo 5.1). Due to relatively short investment recovery time and good rental income, this type of housing helps owners to build apartments in the absence of external financing. Almost all the households (99 per cent) plan to build their apartments with six storeys or up to the maximum height permitted by building bylaws (Photo 5.2). The buildings therefore need a strong foundation, which is often provided in the form of deep pile foundations. Cast-in-situ piles are widely used, involving substantial investment as well as construction time. Thus, in phase C, the households acquire fairly good construction skills, including sub-soil investigations and foundation building. After completing the foundation works, the households raise the land up to plinth level (about 0.5 m higher than maximum flood level) by sand filling.

In phase D, the households start to build grade beams, columns, and brick works. Once the brick works are complete, people then try to cast the roof slabs, which constitutes phase E. Depending on affordability, practicality, and

Photo 5.1 L-shaped semi-permanent house

Mohamed Kamruzzaman

Photo 5.2 Piecemeal (left) and non-piecemeal (right) development

Mohamed Kamruzzaman

expediency, people cast either whole or partial roof slabs. Within the study area, both of the following were common practices: 1) casting half of the roof and quickly finishing the interior; and 2) casting the entire roof and then finishing the interior over a longer period of time. After casting the roof slabs, the owners move into their semi-finished houses and then gradually complete the remaining work by self labour (phase F). During the next stage, the owners complete the remaining portions of the same floor for their tenants, who are then invited to move in (phase G). The households then take a break from building and save money to prepare for subsequent construction works, which constitute phase H.

After this time-out period, people start by casting staircases, columns, and brickwork for the next floor. Again, with the addition of another floor, households must decide whether to cast the entire roof or just half a roof (phase I). As the interior finishing requires additional financing, people often do this incrementally (phase J) and often floors are left incomplete until funding is found. Again, given favourable situations and time, households continue building subsequent floors. Meanwhile, the households attain good construction skills as well as bulk rental income, which they utilize to construct subsequent floors. In later stages, the pace of construction is faster than in the initial stages, given the acquired skills of the owner-builders in both construction and in obtaining funding. The households continue building until all the floors are finished according to the master plan. Funding remains the main obstacle with regard to increasing the pace of construction. Owner-builders of different educational, professional, and social backgrounds gradually acquire construction skills during the construction of their buildings and were found to be adequately satisfied and experienced by the end of construction. Thus, self-help piecemeal construction remains a popular housing construction style in Bangladesh.

Timeframe of piecemeal development

The time required to complete construction projects can be determined by establishing a timeframe or breaking the entire construction works down into specific incremental steps over time. However, accomplishing the latter task proves difficult in practice. The fuel for construction is money, and hence the pace of construction depends directly on the availability of funding. Households manage the money for their construction projects in the face of variable and individual circumstances. Thus, construction time varies widely from household to household. To give a time-based sequence of construction, we can take Golam Mohammad's house (from Part 3) as an example from among the 1,089 surveyed housing plots. Mr Mohammad bought his plot in 1982 and finished building a four-storey apartment in 2005, thus spanning a total of 23 years. He has no desire to build additional floors. As the construction projects of other households show no significant disparities with this example, a project could be said to require an estimated 20 to 25 years to complete.

Informal developers

Multi-storey apartments are being built by the public sector, formal private developers, and self-help owner-builders in the study area. Details of the development profiles of the three providers are presented in Figure 5.3. Only five public apartments were found in Part 1 of the study area, while the other three parts had no public apartments. Part 1 also showed a good number of apartments that were built by private formal developers. This can be explained by the fact that the lots of Part 1 are relatively large, making them more suitable for large apartment buildings than smaller houses. Yet, as owner-builders are generally unable to build these apartments with their own funding, they sell their land to formal developers, who then build the apartments.

Self-help owner-builders comprised the largest group of housing providers in the study area. About 92.6 per cent of all apartments in the RRA were built by owner-builders; and in smaller plots, this percentage was above 98 per cent. This group includes both piecemeal developers and non-piecemeal developers. As a whole, piecemeal developers contributed 71.1 per cent of apartments in the RRA, with 21.5 per cent of all apartments belonging to non-piecemeal developers (see Figure 5.4).

Housing consolidation through informal construction

There are many paths leading from small, temporary, one-room, un-serviced dwellings to larger, permanent, multi-room, fully-serviced dwellings. Many houses are slowly but steadily consolidated in an incremental way, with rooms added gradually and facilities upgraded as income allows. Other houses, such as semi-permanent dwellings, often remain static and receive little more than

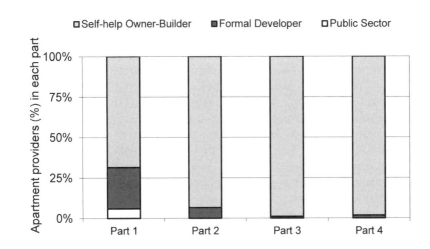

Figure 5.3 Apartments provided by the different providers in the RRA

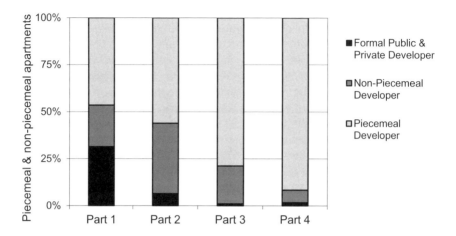

Figure 5.4 Apartments provided by piecemeal and non-piecemeal providers

basic maintenance. Some houses remain at the same stage for long periods, but when the opportunity arrives, are consolidated quickly and effectively. A small minority of households are able to finance the construction of a completed dwelling within a short period. The various stages of house consolidation can be characterized as temporary, semi-permanent, developing, and completing (see Figure 5.2). Because of the continuous and incremental nature of most construction, it is rare to find dwellings that are regarded by their owners as completed.

This section examines the interrelationship between self-help construction activities and the consolidation of the houses. Most self-help builders have little surplus income and obtaining construction loans is difficult. Possible alternative strategies for raising money to finance a construction are renting out the dwelling units and taking out sizable informal loans. The importance of renting as a means to finance further construction has been widely recognized (Gilbert, 1987; Rakodi, 1995). There is thus a direct relationship between the level of consolidation of the settlement and the extent to which the rental units are rented out. Table 5.1 is an estimate of the output of the interviewed building firms in the study area. Table 5.1 shows that 70 per cent of the interviewed firms completed about 8,000 to 10,000 ft² of construction within one year – a remarkable feat. It is assumed that almost 70 per cent of this new construction is for rental use.

Table 5.2 presents the housing consolidation level in the settlement as a whole. Longitudinal fieldwork done over three consecutive years traced the changes in housing types and the development scale. A first field survey in the study area, conducted in 2006, made an inventory of the total housing stock,

Table 5.1 Building firms' output in one year

Floor area (ft²)	Number of firms	Percentage
< 2,000	2	10
2,000– 4,000	3	15
6,000–8,000	1	5
8,000–10,000	14	70

Table 5.2 Percentage of housing in each consolidation stage in the settlement sites

Stage of consolidation	Part 1		Part 2		Part 3		Part 4	
	2006	2009	2006	2009	2006	2009	2006	2009
Temporary	12	11	8	7	2	1	3	2
Semi-permanent	52	47	24	20	25	18	59	51
Developing	25	30	41	44	58	63	36	43
Completing	11	12	27	29	15	18	2	4

type, and number of rental units. In a consecutive survey in 2009, the physical changes were traced. Table 5.2 shows that, on average, 2 per cent of housing structures of the study area were built within three years.

Most households in self-help settlements such as the RRA are able to consolidate their homes over time. As the houses become more consolidated, so does their potential to generate rental income, which can then be further invested in completing the construction. The processes concerning financing, construction, and generating rental income are continually changing. As shown in Table 5.2, the average housing development scale has risen in all of the settlements in the RRA. Table 5.2 also shows how over a three-year period, the average level of consolidation increased in all settlements. It also shows how in Part 3, houses transition quite rapidly from the development to the completion stage.

Conclusions

This chapter corroborates the consensus that housing construction practices of cities in the Global South are different in nature and scope from those in developed countries. It presents the findings of a field survey conducted in a typical area in the capital of Bangladesh in order to explore culturally rooted housing construction practices. The survey illustrated that households are intimately involved in the process of creating and controlling building construction. The owner-builders divide the construction process into smaller tasks and then construct the building using a piecemeal approach. They first build their own dwelling units and then build additional units for rental use depending on affordability, practicality, and expediency. About 90 per cent of all apartments were produced through informal efforts. In later stages, construction speed is faster than in the initial stage due to the owner-builders gaining construction skills as well as experience in finding sources of informal finance. At the end of construction, owner-builders were found to be adequately satisfied and experienced. It takes on average 20 to 25 years to bring a house to full completion.

In the Global South, the role of informal housing providers as producers of shelter has been overlooked. As a result, the critical role these providers play in supplying housing has been neither exposed nor supported. Formal providers tend to build housing specifically as rental property. Informal providers, by contrast, are more apt to use existing property when developing rental units. The significance of this distinction lies in government policy, which aims to support the supply of rental housing for urban poor tenants and informal providers. If policies are implemented to support mass housing, then they should focus less on formal providers and more on informal providers, as it is the latter group that has been consistently supplying shelter for the poor. Efforts to improve housing policies and to increase the informal building capacity in cities in the Global South would thus do well to investigate and consider the role and strategies of informal providers of housing.

Notes

1   Apart from squatter settlements, self-help housing is also manifested by the illegal subdivision of land in urban peripheral areas (Gilbert and Ward, 1985).
2   An aerial photograph of the study area can be found at http://wikimapia.org/839072/
3   To establish a typical model of a piecemeal construction process in Dhaka City, we used the degree of completion of construction works and the degree of construction experience as comparative benchmarks. This is an estimate and both the parameters are unitless. Models of these kinds can be found in Payne (2001), for further reference.

References

Ahmed, I. (1998) 'Crisis of natural building materials and institutionalized self-help housing: The case of Grameen Bank in Bangladesh', *Habitat International* 22(4): 355–74.

BBS (Bangladesh Bureau of Statistics) (1988) 'Households and housing structure in Bangladesh: Evidences from a demographic sample survey 1982', BBS, Dhaka.

Gilbert, A. G. (1987) 'Latin America's urban poor: Shanty dwellers or renters of rooms?', *Cities* 4(1): 43–51.

Gilbert, A. G. and Ward, P. (1985) *Housing, the State and the Poor: Policy and Practice in Latin American Cities*, Cambridge University Press, Cambridge.

Okpala, D. C. I. (1992) 'Housing production systems and technologies in developing countries: A review of the experiences and possible future trends/prospects', *Habitat International* 16(3): 9–32.

Payne, G. (2001) 'Urban land tenure policy options: Titles or rights?', *Habitat International* 25(3): 415–29.

Rakodi, C. (1995) 'Rental tenure in the cities of developing countries', *Urban Studies* 32(4–5): 791–811.

Tipple, G. A. (1994) 'A matter of interface: The need for a shift in targeting housing intervention', *Habitat International* 18(4): 1–15.

Turner, J. F. C. (1976) *Housing by People*, Marion Boyars Publishers Ltd, London.

UNCHS (Habitat) (1996) *The Istanbul Declaration and Habitat II Agenda*, UNCHS, Istanbul.

World Bank (1993) *Housing: Enabling Markets to Work*, World Bank Washington DC.

About the author

Mohamed Kamruzzaman is an assistant professor in the Department of Civil Engineering at Rajshahi University of Engineering and Technology (RUET) in Rajshahi, Bangladesh. He holds a bachelor's degree in civil engineering from the Department of Civil Engineering at RUET and master's and doctoral degrees in architectural planning from the University of the Ryukyus, Japan. His current teaching and research focuses on housing design strategies for low-income and disaster-prone communities. He is a member of the Architectural Institute of Japan and has several publications to his credit. He is also a practising architect who has produced a significant body of built work.

Chapter 6

Socio-spatial tensions and interactions: An ethnography of the condominium housing of Addis Ababa, Ethiopia

Alazar G. Ejigu

Abstract

In the city of Addis Ababa, Ethiopia, an ambitious government programme has tried to reduce the country's severe housing shortage through the large-scale production of low-cost condominium housing. This study examines the interactive relationship between the residents' way of life and the spatial organization and spatial quality of this housing project. Different motivations and expectations were held by all stakeholders: politicians, planners, and residents (who may be either tenants or owners). Based on ethnographic surveys and key-person interviews, the study discusses how these expectations and attempts for fulfilment continuously influence spatial use, and hence the functional and social performance of the housing estate. While most studies on similar housing programmes are conducted years after the implementation of the programme, this study focuses on the processes as they evolve over time.

Introduction

Like many other countries, Ethiopia has been faced with a severe housing shortage as a result of rapid urbanization. And also like many other countries, it has tried to solve this problem by applying the modernist 'provider model', comprised of strong public-sector involvement in the centralized construction of ready-made, minimum-standard units for anonymous residents. In recent years, an ambitious government programme for low-cost condominium housing resulted in the construction of hundreds of thousands of walk-up apartment blocks nationwide and in several thousand housing units in the city of Addis Ababa alone.

The incompatibility of modernist housing solutions with the lifestyles and aspirations of the poor has been a persistent concern among architects and planners for many years. While direct government provision of low-cost housing does exist in most countries in the Global South, these programmes generally fail to meet the social and cultural needs of the poor. For example, most policies and programmes are insensitive to the diverse needs of target groups, which are often too broadly defined (Turner, 1980; Hamdi, 1991).

Despite the volume of studies and arguments made against the modernist housing model, the approach continues to persist across housing practices and policies. This results in a continuation of the misalignment between the physical form of the housing and the lifestyles of major segments of the inhabitants.

This chapter discusses how the interactive relationship between the residents' way of life and the spatial organization of condominium housing influences spatial use, and hence the functional and social performance of the housing estate. While most studies on similar housing programmes are generally conducted years after the implementation of the housing programme in question, this study observes and examines processes as they evolve over time as well as the ways in which residents adapt to or reject the physical and social environments of the housing units they live in. Understanding such processes is vital to the design and development of housing for low-income people.

The Grand Housing Program

In 2004, the Grand Housing Program (GHP) was introduced in Addis Ababa to reduce the overwhelming housing backlog, estimated at about 300,000 housing units, and to replace 50 per cent of the overall 136,330 dilapidated public rental houses (locally known as '*kebele*' houses[1]) (AACA, 2005). A main feature of the GHP is that the housing units were sold to the inhabitants as condominiums[2] rather than being rented. The ambitious plan also sought to address a number of other problems of the city, including high unemployment and the low level of skills in the construction sector. The municipal government set itself the goal of constructing between 40,000 and 50,000 low-cost houses per year over five years (AAHDPO, 2007; City Government, 2008). By 2007, the national government had scaled up the programme to cover 36 cities, and by 2008 to cover 59 cities (MWUD, 2008). In Addis Ababa, however, only about 60,000 housing units had been built, and of those, only 36,000 had been transferred to owners by February 2009 (*The Reporter*, 2009; AAHDPO, 2007).

The condominiums are designed in blocks of three- to five-storey buildings, containing one- to three-room housing units, with some blocks having four-room housing units on the upper floors and commercial space on the ground floors. The blocks have four basic modular typologies: A, B, C (Photo 6.1), and D that exist at several scales with little variation.

For every three to five blocks, one common room is also built in which activities such as cooking with fire wood, animal slaughtering, clothes washing, and social gatherings can take place. Presently, condominium blocks in Addis Ababa are distributed over 100 locations, most of which are in the inner city. The number of blocks in each location varies, ranging from 1 to over 100. A recent proposal by the Addis Ababa Housing Development Project

Alazar G. Ejigu

Photo 6.1 Exterior view of condominium block – Type C

Office (AAHDPO) (2009) also states plans to build 8- to 31-storey condominium blocks.

In 2006, only one year after the transfer of the first condominium units to residents, and 10 years since John Turner's concept of 'supporters' (i.e. the 'enabling strategy') had become an integral part of the vocabulary of official documents,[3] UN-Habitat added the GHP of Addis Ababa to its best practices database (UN-Habitat, 2006). The use of 'cost and time efficient technology', 'supply of enough land without displacing residents', 'facilitating the creation and organization of 1566 Micro & Small Enterprises for the production' of housing blocks, and 'creating more than 40,000 jobs' are the reasons given for why the Ethiopian housing model was considered a 'best practice' (UN-Habitat, 2006). Given these acclaimed achievements, the grandness of the programme's scale, the ensuing debate among planners and politicians about the appropriateness of the GHP, and above all the pressing need for housing for the urban poor throughout the world make the study of this case relevant. Furthermore, most studies on modernist housing have been conducted years after the housing complexes in question were developed. The young age of the housing programme of Addis Ababa, coupled with its consistent building form, make it a valuable case for studying the processes that bring residents to either adapt to or reject a housing complex over time.

The main purpose of my ongoing doctoral research, only a part of which is summarized in this chapter, is to analyse the relationship between the way of life (also defined as 'lifestyle'[4] in the study) of identified groups of residents and the spatial organization and spatial quality of the built condominiums of Addis Ababa. As this relationship is mutually interactive, the study attempts to find out if and how different activities and social functions are supported, or impeded, by the nature of the physical environment and, conversely, how the spaces and facilities are used and transformed by dwellers to meet local demands.

The main objective of the doctoral study is to evaluate and develop a more coherent operational view of architecture and planning as a social support instrument for the design and planning of cost-conscious, large-scale, multi-family housing environments. In so doing, it intends to raise awareness and improve understanding among planners and politicians about alternative ways to create functional housing for the poor. In an effort to meet this objective, the policy implications of the study's findings will be forwarded to pertinent planners and politicians in Addis Ababa.

People's way of life and the built environment

There is ample evidence of a close linkage between people's way of life and the design of buildings (e.g. Rapoport, 1969). The strong tie between space and 'social morphology' is extensively discussed in Oliver's *Encyclopedia of Vernacular Architecture of the World* (Oliver, 1999). New social structures often demand new spaces, either for 'flows or places' (Castells, 1996), and in a similar manner, new spaces may facilitate or discourage existing social relations or may initiate the development of new ones. Nevertheless, politicians and planners often do not take lifestyles into consideration, or assume that lifestyles will adapt to the built environment. However, studies have shown that behaviour does not always change easily, or that, even when it does change, quality of life is not improved (Holston, 1989).

Housing for the urban poor: Modernism vs. the vernacular

The drive behind the extensive spread of apartment blocks in most countries in the Global South, as seen in the prefabrication and standardization of building elements, was to increase efficiency and reduce costs. However, evidence shows that, at least in low- and middle-income countries, such procedures actually increase costs (Tipple, 2000). The scarcity of land and material resources and the desire for cleaner and more 'orderly' living environments are the main arguments for replacing informal settlements (largely characterized by single-storey temporary structures) with standardized medium- and high-rise buildings.

The modernist housing model is criticized above all for its poor social and functional outputs and the economic challenges it often poses for low-income households. The failure of the model has been well documented by various scholars (e.g. Holston, 1989). The inappropriateness of modernist apartment blocks is evidenced by the fact that such housing areas are often transformed incrementally by illegal or semi-legal extensions. For many people, such transformations constitute an alternative to moving out when household demands change. Transformations also serve to personalize one's own environment, thereby increasing residents' attachment to their housing environment (Tipple, 2000).

In recent years, scholars have suggested alternative strategies based on vernacular housing design methods (e.g. Anh, 1999; Abbaszadeh et al., 2009). Studies have also explored spatial qualities that are absent in the formally planned modernist housing areas but that are found to exist in unplanned informal settlements (Correa, 1985; Tipple, 2000). However, very few attempts have been made to transfer this understanding into the design of planned areas.

Despite the growing concern over the inefficiency of the GHP condominium housing developments in Ethiopia, no in-depth study has been carried out on the social and socio-cultural performance of this type of housing. The few studies made recently on GHP either focus exclusively on issues of affordability or their technical performance (e.g. AAHDPO, 2005; CRDA, 2007) or make vary general assessments of social housing programmes in general (e.g. Abiy, 2006; Routh, 2006; Bisrat, 2008).

Pilot study

A number of studies on the relationships between built environments and people highlight the complexity of the subject and its attendant methodological challenges. They hold, for example, that any improvement would require coping with a broader range of physical, historical, and behavioural issues. To develop a more meaningful combination of methods and strategies for the main field study, and to develop relevant lines of questions for the study as a whole, I began with a pilot study following recommendations made by expert researchers (Yin, 2003; Bryman, 2008).

The study examined eight condominium housing sites in Addis Ababa, selected to accommodate differences in size, location, and length of occupation. It involved the application of multiple methods, including direct observation, document analyses of the housing complexes, and in-depth interviews with 35 mainly randomly selected residents as well as with well-informed planners and housing agency officials. House owners, tenants, female-headed households, and families with and without children were represented in the sample of interviewees.

The methods used in the pilot field study proved useful for collecting background information. However, other information, such as the uses made of space as well as behavioural and attitudinal issues, was difficult to obtain or understand without a much closer involvement with the people and without access to the more intimate spaces of their dwellings. To remedy this problem, participant observation was used as the primary mode of data collection in the main field study. The usefulness of participant observation for studying interpersonal behaviours and people's established customs and rules, their hidden desires and ambitions, and their conflicts and harmonies is discussed by various authors (e.g. Davies, 1999; Yin, 2003). The usefulness of participant observation specifically for housing research has also been discussed by several researchers (e.g. Kellet and Tipple, 2005; Vestbro, 2005).

Ethnographic survey

Literature on the subject of ethnography highlights the conflicting task of the researcher as the detached, objective observer on the one hand and the more subjective, participating observer on the other hand (e.g. Davies, 1999; Have, 2004; Hume and Mulcock, 2005; Vestbro, 2005). The challenges often arise from the following circumstances: 1) the deliberate attempt, by the researcher, to simultaneously position him- or herself as both insider and outsider; 2) the difficulty of avoiding subjectivity in the role of 'objective' researcher; and 3) the diverse ethical issues raised when having to make choices at various points in the study process. It is also possible that the complex nature of the objects of this study, for example the hardly understood concept of 'space' and its reciprocal relationship with humans, makes it even more difficult to apply a method. Further challenges that avail in applying ethnographic methods to study housing environments have been documented by other authors (e.g. Holston, 1989; Vestbro, 2005).

In early December 2009, I moved with my family into one of the oldest condominium housing areas in Addis Ababa. There, I carried out a participant observation of condominium living lasting four months, which was in line with Vestbro's (2005) suggestion for an appropriate time duration for such studies. To make my observation representative (in terms of size and location) and to make it sufficiently manageable, I selected this housing area, consisting of six condominium blocks and located in a fairly well-serviced area between the city centre and the perimeter of the city.

I made my observations at different times of the day every day. Often I would return home several times a day to take short notes, and in the evening I would sit for a few hours to meditate and write down my observations and experiences – all in the form of a detailed diary. As time went by, what first appeared as fragmented bits of information then began to take form. Much of the analysis of the data was thus made during the field study.

Some methodological findings

My experience as a participant observer revealed a number of valuable methodological insights that are only selectively presented in this chapter. The traditional approach in most ethnographic studies involves cohabiting with a family in the community being studied. One key methodological finding in my field survey regards the strategic choice I made to move into the condominium housing with my family as opposed to living in the same dwelling with another family. As it turned out, I became better known to people accompanied as I was with my wife and young daughter than had I come alone. Apart from making people less suspicious of me and my research, my daughter often served as a means to get me in touch with people, and my wife literally became my research assistant by bringing me useful information through her informal channels. It was clear that most of the women in the housing area found it easier to communicate their concerns, fears, and ambitions to my wife than to me, regardless of whether I approached them informally as a neighbour or formally as a researcher with formal enquiries.

The field study also demonstrated how a considerable level of trust can be achieved by starting out this kind of work as a participant within the community and then gradually transitioning to taking on the role of researcher. For the first month and a half, I made it a habit to take my daughter and sit for hours in the common yard 'watching my daughter' and not interfering in any way, all the while, of course, engaged in passive observation. People from all floors and nearly all blocks could see us. Within a few weeks, many people began to recognize me and my daughter.

A downside of my field study was that a planned complementary questionnaire survey that was supposed to gather factual information about other condominium housing areas could not be conducted due to time and resource limitations. To offset this loss, two strategies are currently being considered for the continuation of this study: the use of secondary data from the number of academic and institutional research papers recently produced in the case areas; and, to achieve more persuasive and high-quality results, the completion of a supplementary field survey based on a well-designed questionnaire survey to fill missing gaps and to compare results with other condominium sites and possibly with other housing complexes.

Views, expectations, and attempts for fulfilment

The examination of views about the GHP housing programme presupposed three main groups of actors: the government, the planners and architects, and the condominium residents. The way in which these housing complexes were described by the different actors gave insight into the motivations of each actor, in turn providing an indication as to their respective actions that played a role in the early or continued shaping of the built form.

Regardless of who benefited from the housing and how appropriate the blocks are for the beneficiaries, the general attitude about the condominium project appeared to be positive among all three groups. However, differences in views became apparent by means of a more in-depth investigation assisted by ethnographic interviews and discussions on different aspects of the housing, such as the physical form of the buildings, the space and its use, and issues concerning lifestyle and culture.

The idea of providing 'affordable housing' through 'low-cost construction technology' and 'subsidies' is strongly embraced by the government, as disclosed in interviews with officials and through official documents. The planners, for their part, place great emphasis on 'efficient use of land' through 'increasing population density' and 'vertical building'. A further concept is the ambition to make Addis Ababa into 'the capital of Africa' by building the 'modern city'. Although not openly professed in the interviews, this vision was expressed in various articles, official documents, and other media publications (e.g. ECA, 2009). Condominium blocks, given their standardized design and formalized planning, are considered by the government and the general public as an important part of creating a 'modern city'. The general belief is that shortly or with time, people will adapt to 'the modern way of life' that the condominiums offer. This assumption is apparent from the 'Regulations and Rules for Condominium Residents' document (AAHDPO, 2008), which, with its detailed 'dos and don'ts', aspires for an attitudinal change among the people. Such urges for adaptation to the new life are also indirectly but insistently implied in other official documents, newspapers, study reports, and the media (Routh, 2006; AAHDPO, 2008; *The Reporter*, 2009).

On the whole, observations made during the study indicate that expectations have not been met. For example, the current attempt by the government to educate residents on the use of private and shared spaces has not been successful (MWUD, 2008). However, evidence does exist that residents are indeed changing their way of life to some extent, although often at additional cost to them. For example, many residents have been forced to stop buying live sheep,[5] especially during holidays, because of the lack of space in the housing area to keep them. As a result, residents increasingly turn to having the sheep slaughtered at the location where they buy them,[6] which costs the residents not only more money for slaughtering but also for transportation, as the meat then has to be transported to the housing unit. The trend also marks an important shift from a cultural and spatial perspective.

Although the residents' general impression of condominium housing is positive, differences with regard to intentions and expectations were observed between tenants and owners. Depending on the location, reports and other studies indicate that the percentage of tenants in condominium houses, i.e. those who rent rather than own the units, averages between 40 per cent and 60 per cent (Bisrat, 2008; Lohnert and Fein, 2008; AAHDPO, 2009). Generally, tenants seemed more critical of life in condominium housing than owners, and showed less tolerance of problems in the housing area. In the studied areas, tenants generally did not participate in the development and management of their housing areas and had little or no involvement in the local traditional saving associations called *iddirs*.[7] The implications of this lack of participation by tenants in the sustained development of the housing environments are enormous.

Owners, by contrast, viewed condominium housing as the best available means to own an asset, in particular for diversifying their source of income by renting out their housing unit or, when conditions allow, by selling it at a great profit. At the moment, a law prohibits owners of GHP condominiums from selling their units within the first five years of entitlement. Asked where they see themselves in 5, 10, and 15 years, about half of the owners said that they would no longer want to be there in 10 years. Some of the interviewed owners not living in the condominium area indicated a great interest to live in their own housing unit, but often expressed a fear of the economic insecurity they could face after moving in.

The situation is not much different for tenants. In the housing area subjected to an ethnographic study, comprising 250 households, there was on average one household moving out each week. With a roughly estimated tenant rate of 50 per cent, the average time a tenant stays in the condominium housing was calculated to be a little over two years.

In line with Turner's (1980) theory on priorities of the poor with respect to housing, the location of the condominiums was shown to be one of its most highly valued aspects. The location brings economic and practical advantages to the residents in terms of better transport and access to public services. Moreover, as the condominium blocks are centrally located, they can generate high rents, giving owners the option to rent out their units rather than living in them. This is reflected in the higher rents and the low vacancy rates of the condominiums located closer to the city centre and the lower rents and higher vacancy rates of those located on the outskirts. The Mikyliland[8] condominium site, for example, although one of the most complete and well-serviced housing areas with well-built streets and other infrastructure, has the highest vacancy due to its suburban location.

How is condominium housing viewed by neighbours and the general public? The study indicated that there is a tendency among people living in neighbouring housing areas to see condominium residents as invaders. However, this view is counterbalanced by the fact that the condominiums create significant business opportunities for neighbouring residents. Some condominium residents felt that they were being seen as outsiders because they came from different parts of the city, having been picked by a 'government lottery system'.[9] Cases of verbal and physical attacks by people from adjacent housing areas were also reported at some condominium sites. The situation was a bit different in areas where people from the local area lived in the condominium houses.

Social-spatial interactions[10]

The study of the relationship between neighbours in the housing area indicated the varying degrees of relational unease that abides among certain types of residents, such as between: tenants and other residents who are owners; maids and housewives; and households with different economic statuses. A relational unease was even noted among residents with regard to the floors they lived on. People on the ground floor tended to be critical of those living on the upper floors with regard to problems such as noise, water leakage incidents, and lack of cleanliness. The study showed that much of the tension can be led back to functional, technical, and management problems inherent in the design and construction of the buildings. One of these problems is that condominium blocks are constructed by builders who, to accelerate job creation under GHP, receive only brief, rudimentary training.

In most cases, more interaction also meant more conflict and unease. For example, the conflicts between maids and housewives were directly related to the fact that they are the main users of the shared spaces for washing and drying clothes. This results in continuous competition for control over adjacent spaces in the housing area as well as a continuous struggle to define and claim territory by way of using it frequently (Photo 6.2a) and putting private belongings on it for extended periods of time (Photo 6.2b). In this way, households appropriate spaces and assume de facto ownership over them.

There is evidence that people become deprived of certain social benefits, many of which have direct economic implications, by moving from housing estates with well-established communities, such as those with *kebele* houses and old settlements with mixed tenures, to condominium housing. One such benefit concerns how children are raised in more traditional housing settlements. There, long-term neighbours, friends, and nearby relatives all keep an eye on children as they run around, and otherwise engage in sharing the responsibility of supervising children in the absence of the parents. By contrast, in condominium housing, there is less possibility for the close supervision of children by relatives and members of the community. One explanation for this is that condominium housing estates are too young for such a community support network to develop. Some also blame the lottery system, which, allocating the housing units to beneficiaries on a random basis, does not give resettlers the choice of moving close to where former neighbours moved.

In theory, shared spaces and facilities should allow for a better possibility for social interaction and relationship-building. However, in practice this is not always provided. On the contrary, the results of the study show that many people defied the suggested behavioural adaptations expected from their new physical environment. For example, the highly transparent building form, with its open and shared corridors and staircases, along with the spatial layout of the courtyard, impose an extreme openness on the residents, especially considering that these have been 'thrown together', so to speak, by the lottery system. As a result, the inhabitants try to reclaim their privacy by avoiding contact with neighbours and by keeping behind closed doors. They thus avoid engaging in social engagements or meetings, seeking rather to establish and nurture their social network outside of the housing complex.

Alazar G. Ejigu

Alazar G. Ejigu

Photo 6.2 Attempts to define territory through a) frequent use of a space; and b) putting private belongings in shared spaces

Conclusions

This chapter examined the social functioning of condominium housing in Addis Ababa. By analysing how views, expectations, and attempts for fulfilment continuously influence the spatial use, and hence the social and functional development of the housing environment, it tried to build a general understanding of the socio-spatial dynamic that exists in large-scale, multi-family housing environments.

The study briefly highlighted the social and physical inadequacies that can arise in housing environments when planners and politicians, swayed either by excessive idealism or rationalism, fail to take into account the key factors that sustain the continuous development of a housing environment. It also showed how unintended results become inevitable when people moving into a housing area are motivated primarily by outcomes that are different from those targeted or anticipated by the provider. It is thus fair to conclude that in the provider model, the housing development process is largely shaped by the less explicit desires and motivations of both parties involved, here the residents and the providers. In the studied case, the housing provider veered from the initial task of providing standard housing by pursuing grandiose visions of a 'modern city' that were ultimately fuelled by the desire for commercial profit. This clashed with the motivations of the beneficiaries, who, for their part, initially sought only decent housing, but later came to seek added economic value by renting or selling their condominium units.

The condominiums of Addis Ababa, like most other modernist housing, are designed for a broad and loosely defined category of low- to middle-income users, without sufficient attention paid to the differences that exist within that group. In this study, this lack of differentiation in the conceptual design manifested in the prevailing tendency among residents to vie for control over adjacent spaces, while at the same time closing themselves off socially to avoid conflicts.

Despite the brave and commendable attempt to address the multiple problems of the urban poor, the case of Addis Ababa's GHP demonstrates the additional challenges that result when trying to solve urban problems with 'package solutions'. Unless accompanied by a thorough understanding of the complex relationship between the elements being introduced, such attempts can only be expected to yield unintended results.

The lessons learned are clear: long-term objectives, and not radical and instant-solution approaches, must accompany even modest efforts to tackle multiple problems. Planners and politicians need to gain a more realistic and precise understanding of the life of the urban poor, and integrate that understanding into their architectural projects and policies. Planners and decision-makers must also understand that the urban poor have a complex web of social networks and that their multi-faceted problems cannot be successfully addressed with a simplistic model. Planners must approach building as a process and abandon the mechanical, reductionist view that aims for an ideal, if not utopian, end product. Such a process calls for incremental development strategies and a more direct partnership with the community.

The insights gained from this case study challenge the common assumption that, in seeking housing solutions for the urban poor, building standardized housing blocks for a loosely defined category of 'average users' brings economic advantages. 'Neutral' housing environments that serve the 'average user' do not appear to deliver the desired results, suggesting the need for a greater differentiation of the users, for example according to family size, age group, religious background, or spatial needs. For future research, the various housing models could also be studied from perspectives guided by democratic values and sustainability principles.

Notes

1   *Kebele* houses are generally single-storey mud and wood houses and constitute approximately 70 per cent of the housing stock in the central parts of the city. With their very low rents and favourable locations, they are the best available option for the low- and lowest-income households that comprise the majority in the city.

2   In the Ethiopian context, as in the USA and many provinces of Canada, the term 'condominium', or 'condo', refers to an apartment that the resident owns or is entitled to as opposed to one that is rented. It is generally used to refer to the form of housing tenure under the GHP, where each apartment unit is individually owned, while use of and access to common facilities is controlled by the owners, who, through an association, jointly represent ownership of the entire property.

3   Turner's concept of 'supporters' officially appeared for the first time in the documents of UN-Habitat at the Habitat II conference in Istanbul in 1996. The concept was subsequently discussed further and came to be referred to as the 'enabling strategy' (e.g. Hamdi, 1991).

4   The word 'lifestyle' is used with a limited definition referring to the social and cultural dimensions of living that reflect the attitudes, values, and aspirations of people.

5   Mostly as a way to ensure household food security or as a means to generate additional income, micro-scale urban farming, including raising chickens inside the house, is a common practice in urban Ethiopia. Lamb is an expensive food that most people cannot afford to buy except for special occasions or holidays. On such occasions, people usually keep and feed the sheep in the housing yard for a few days before slaughtering it before or on the day of the occasion or holiday.

6   This trend could change once the 'communal blocks', within which a place for slaughtering is allocated, are made accessible for residents.

7   *Iddir* (also spelled *idir*, *eddir*, or *edir*) are voluntary saving associations often formed by residents of or in proximity to a neighbourhood for supporting one another in times of difficulty.

8   A suburban housing area located in the west of Addis Ababa. With 4,000 housing units, this condominium site is one of the largest of the city.

9 The lottery system is conducted by the housing project office and allocates housing units to potential beneficiaries on a random lottery basis. In this way, it gives beneficiaries no chance to express preferences with regard to location. The system is monitored by representatives of other public institutions and the media.

10 Studies that are, or that could be, referred to as 'socio-spatial' are common in the fields of sociology, anthropology, geography, psychology, and architecture. In this chapter, the terms 'socio-spatial' and 'housing' have the conventional meanings they hold in the field of architecture, where user experience and functional, spatial, and design aspects of the built environment are more central than, for instance, financial and planning aspects. Moreover, 'space' is understood as the vacancy that is left by physical forms in the built environment and is defined by the activities taking place within it.

References

AACB (Addis Ababa City Administration (2005) 'Addis Ababa', Addis Ababa City Administration, Addis Ababa.

AAHDPO (Addis Ababa Housing Development Project Office) (2005) 'A study conducted around the utilization of a condominium building by those residents who are dwelling at the Gerji Model Houses', Land Preparation, Infrastructure Development and Design Department, Addis Ababa Housing Development Project Office, Addis Ababa.

AAHDPO (2007) 'Integrated Housing Development Programme: Undergoing projects and components that require support', prepared for potential donors, Addis Ababa Housing Development Project Office, Addis Ababa.

AAHDPO (2008) 'Rules, regulations and guides for association of condominium owners', official document written in Amharic, Addis Ababa Housing Development Project Office, Addis Ababa.

AAHDPO (2009) 'Low cost housing', proposed architectural drawings, Addis Ababa Housing Development Project Office, Addis Ababa.

Abbaszadeh, S., Ibrahim, R., Baharuddin, M., and Salim, A. (2009) 'Identifying Persian traditional socio-cultural behaviors for application in the design of modern high-residences', *Archnet-IJAR, International Journal of Architectural Research* 3(3): 116–32.

Abiy, W. (2006) 'Housing and the urban poor through condominium housing', project case study of the Gerji pilot project, bole sub-city, kebele 11, Department of Geography and Environmental Studies, College of Social Sciences, Addis Ababa University, Addis Ababa.

Anh, T. H. (1999) *Another Modernism? Form, Content and Meaning of the New Housing Architecture of Hanoi*, University of Lund Publication, Lund.

Bisrat, K. (2008) 'Public housing: The condominium approach, the case of Addis Ababa', Master's thesis, Addis Ababa University, Faculty of Technology, Addis Ababa.

Bryman, A. (2008) *Social Research Methods*, 3rd edition, Oxford University Press, Oxford.

Castells, M. (1996) *The Rise of the Network Society. The Information Age: Economy, Society and Culture*, vol. 1, Blackwell Publishers, Malden, MA.

City Government (2008) 'Addis Ababa', www.addisababacity.gov.et/News.htm [accessed 30 March 2008].

Correa, C. (1985) *The New Landscape*, The Book Society of India, Bombay.

CRDA (Christian Relief and Development Association) (2007) *Consequences of the Condominium Housing Project in Addis Ababa with a Focus on Housing Access to the Poorest in the City*, Addis Ababa Civil Society Urban Renewal Committee (ACSURC), CRDA, Addis Ababa.

Davies, C. (1999) *Reflexive Ethnography: A Guide to Researching Selves and Others*, Routledge, London.

ECA (Economic Commission for Africa) (2009) 'Homepage', ECA, www.uneca. org/uncc/ [accessed 30 June 2009].

Hamdi, N. (1991) *Housing Without Houses. Participation, Flexibility, Enablement*, Van Nostrand Reinhold, New York.

Have, P. (2004) *Understanding Qualitative Research and Ethnomethodology*, Sage Publications, London.

Holston, J. (1989) *The Modernist City. An Anthropological Critique of Brasilia*, The University of Chicago Press, Chicago.

Hume, L. and Mulcock, J. (eds) (2005) *Anthropologists in the Field: Cases in Participant Observation*, Columbia University Press, New York.

Kellett, P. and Tipple, G. (2005) 'Researching domestic space and income generation in developing cities', in D. U. Vestbro, Y. Hürol, and N. Wilkinson (eds) *Methodologies in Housing Research*, pp. 206–22, The Urban International Press, Gateshead.

Lohnert, B. and Fein, R. (2008) 'Potentials of different housing strategies – the case of Addis Ababa', Development Studies in Geography, University of Bayreuth, unpublished paper presented at a workshop 12 February, Goethe-Institut, Addis Ababa

MWUD (Ministry of Works and Urban Development) (2008) 'Integrated Housing Development Program of the Federal Democratic Republic of Ethiopia', presented at the African Ministerial Conference on Housing and Urban Development, AMCHUD II, Abuja, Nigeria.

Oliver, P. (1999) *Encyclopedia of Vernacular Architecture of the World*, Cambridge University Press, Cambridge.

Rapoport, A. (1969) *House Form and Culture*, Prentice-Hall, Englewood Cliffs.

Routh, T. (2006) 'Strategy of low-cost housing of Addis-Abeba', Internship report, IUG Institut d'urbanisme, d'aménagement et d'administration territoriale, Addis Ababa.

The Reporter (2009) 'Many condominium owners said unable to settle payment', 28 February, *The Reporter*, http://en.ethiopianreporter.com/index.php?option =com_content&task=view&id=742&Itemid=26 [accessed 15 August 2009].

Tipple, G. (2000) *Extending Themselves. User-initiated Transformations of Government-built Housing in Developing Countries*, Liverpool University Press, Liverpool.

Turner, A. (1980) *The Cities of the Poor – Settlement Planning in Developing Countries*, British Library Cataloguing in Publication Data, London.

UN-Habitat (2006) 'Addis Ababa Grand Housing Development Program', Best Practices Database in Improving the Living Environment, UN-Habitat,

Nairobi, www.unhabitat.org:80/bestpractices/2006/mainview04.asp?BPID=7 [accessed 21 August 2011].

Vestbro, D. U. (2005) 'Participant observation – A method for inside views', in D. U. Vestbro, Y. Hürol, and N. Wilkinson (eds) *Methodologies in Housing Research*, pp. 40–56, The Urban International Press, Gateshead.

Yin, R. (2003) *Case Study Research, Design and Methods*, 3rd edition, Sage Publications, London.

About the author

Alazar G. Ejigu is a PhD candidate at the School of Architecture and Built Environment at the Royal Institute of Technology (KTH), Sweden. He holds a master's degree in built environment with a specialization in spatial planning from KTH, a bachelor's degree in architecture and urban planning from Addis Ababa University, Ethiopia, a certificate in real estate management from KTH, and a certificate in entrepreneurship from the Stockholm School of Entrepreneurship. Alazar has designed a number of private and public buildings in Ethiopia and abroad.

Chapter 7

Partnership modalities for the management of drinking water in poor urban neighbourhoods: The example of Kinshasa, Democratic Republic of Congo

Kamathe Katsongo

Abstract

This research examines partnerships between the public sector and informal operator collectives that contribute to maintaining a constant and reliable water supply to poor urban neighbourhoods. The study was performed in an area on the outskirts of the city of Kinshasa, Congo, and applied the model of Coston (1988). The relationships that corresponded most to the desired partnership were found to be of a 'contracting' type and to have a state-societal orientation, while the water supply management system and power relations currently in place were found to be closer to the 'rivalry' type. The study also shows that partnerships between public actors and informal operator collectives are very difficult to establish outside a solidarity-based socio-political environment. As such, democracy, decentralization, and a strong associative movement carried by civil society were identified as factors that contribute to the desired partnerships.

Introduction

Since the Second World War, economic growth has become a key instrument for consolidating the nation state. Growth theories first evolved in the wake of the work of John Maynard Keynes, who claimed that market mechanisms in developed economies cannot guarantee full-employment equilibrium or prevent structural underemployment of the production capacities and the workforce. It follows, he argued, that it should be the responsibility of the state to compensate for the insufficiencies of the market logic. In the early 1960s, theories assuming that economic growth inevitably leads to overall development led to an impasse, manifested in particular by an increasing disparity of income, especially in the countries of the South. At the same time, the rural exodus, while promoting urbanization and industrialization, also led to severe problems (e.g. unemployment, proliferation of shanty towns, and health problems).

For that reason, many development experts stress that genuine political-economic development benefiting the majority cannot be achieved with a top-down approach by the state, but must be brought about by a bottom-up approach initiated within the informal sector by the populations themselves. Experts moreover argue that such a bottom-up approach is best implemented by non-governmental organizations (NGOs), due to their autonomy with regard to the state and financial institutions, their priorities and organizational modes, their small size, and their non-bureaucratic management style. For this reason, each country must rely on and promote its own strengths, its citizens' participation, the reduction of categorical and spatial disparities, the creation of solidarity networks, and the implementation of decentralized decision-making systems.

In most countries of the Global South, the economic impact of bottom-up projects has been weak, if not non-existent. To date, such projects have failed to create a significant number of new jobs or new sources of income. The main obstacle has been the weak demand for the goods and services produced by these initiatives, given the relatively low growth rate of the formal economy. Moreover, participating NGOs have not put adequate pressure on the authorities or local governments, mainly because they have been hesitant to establish structural relations with the various levels of government and because each organization generally works separately (Sanyal, 1999).

Ultimately, the inherent antagonism between the two modes of development (top-down and bottom-up) proved to be limiting. The top-down development model failed mainly in that it does not consider the specific conditions of each region, while bottom-up development often proved to be too limited in the analysis of the actual conditions required for successfully carrying out initiatives in the field (Vachon, 1993). Therefore structural change through more collaboration between institutions of the formal economy and active groups in the informal sector seems necessary to improve the fight against poverty. At present, our understanding of the modalities of cooperation between the formal economy and the informal social economy is still incomplete (Sanyal, 1999). Therefore, the promotion of interaction between these different spheres of the economy is of crucial importance.

Drinking water supply in the cities of Sub-Saharan Africa

Inefficient or unaffordable infrastructures

The rapid increase of the populations of African cities is not being accompanied by the implementation of additional infrastructures and community facilities. Faced with the exacerbation of the urban crisis, African governments have tried to find solutions. However, since their independencies, their capacity to conceive and implement consistent and coherent policies has continually deteriorated. Bonfiglioli (2003) underlines that, in the case of the decentralization of basic urban services, rural communities lack financial and material resources as well as qualified and motivated personnel, and that relations between rural communities and sectorial ministries are not clearly defined.

The challenges facing local administrations with regard to offering services to citizens have led to recourse to the private sector. However, as a large proportion of the urban African population is extremely poor, this privatization could have negative impacts (Stren and White, 1993). The World Bank (World Bank, 2003) points to the fact that the participation of the private sector in the financing of water and sanitation infrastructures has been met with strong resistance from the populations due to rate increases, which, though aiming to recover costs, have led to an increase of the long-term financial risks (immobilizations). According to UN-Habitat (2005), the poorest urban families cannot even pay the minimum fees required to access infrastructures and basic services.

Emergence of informal operators

The difficulties encountered by the state and the reluctance of the private sector to intervene in poor urban neighbourhoods have led to the emergence of informal operators (private and collective) for the provision of basic urban services. In the drinking water and sanitation sector, a study realized in 10 African cities indicates that, on average, 47 per cent of households turn to small suppliers or traditional sources such as wells for their water needs (Collignon and Vezina, 2000).

Informal operators generally belong to one of two categories. They are independent suppliers who are not affiliated with the public networks, and who may even compete with them. As such, they generally obtain their water from 'alternative' sources, such as their own wells, and distribute it to one water supply point through a piping network or water distribution trucks. Or the informal operators are intermediary suppliers, who expand the already existing public network to non-serviced neighbourhoods. As such, they extend the supply pipeline and control the water supply points or they buy, transport, and deliver the water directly to consumers in exchange for payment (Sansom, 2006). Our study is about this latter category of suppliers, also referred to as 'informal collective suppliers'. They are comprised of civil society organizations involved in community management, such as local NGOs and community organizations.

More generally, informal operators face many constraints, among them inaccessibility to the formal credit system, inaccessibility to land for the installation of infrastructures, insufficient recognition and legal protection, weak means of production, no legal protection of labour, rudimentary and obsolete technologies, recourse to poorly qualified and unstable labour, a reduced scale of operations, and a lack of organization (Hugon, 2003; Maldonado et al., 2004).

Kankwenda et al. (1999) underline that it pays to support solid community organizations. These often fill the vacuum left by inefficient, if not non-existing, public services, and play a capital role in development programmes destined for the poor, in particular due to the spatial coverage that they ensure in underprivileged or remote regions. Nevertheless, their interventions are sporadic, rarely reproducible, and incapable of meeting the full demand for urban services, which often require major investments, especially in the case of drinking water and sanitation. In some sectors, a good number of NGOs are active, often pursuing similar programmes or projects, while in other sectors there are no interventions. Basic services therefore remain inaccessible to many citizens, especially in peripheral zones. According to the United Nations Development Programme (UNDP, 2006), if the current trend continues, Sub-Saharan Africa will not reach the Millennium Development Goal for drinking water until 2040 and for sanitation until 2076.

The example of Kinshasa

In Kinshasa (Democratic Republic of Congo, 7.5 million inhabitants), the percentage of people serviced with water lies at 53 per cent, and daily domestic water consumption oscillates between 15 and 30 litres per day and per inhabitant, dropping down to less than 10 litres in the peripheral neighbourhoods (REGIDESO, 2004). The lack of drinking water leads to the renewed outbreak of diseases, in particular cholera, typhoid fever, bacillary dysentery, diarrhoea, and malaria. It also increases the infant mortality rate considerably. Finally, the degradation of water sources obliges women and girls to cover long distances to meet their water needs.

There is increasing consensus that solutions should be found locally and in the framework of an appropriate collaboration between the state, the private sector, individuals, and civil society. All sectors have their role to play, and that role should be defined at the local level (WHO/UNICEF, 2000). In this study, the objective is to describe, analyse, and explain possible process and partnership mechanisms and to identify the types of partnerships likely to promote the reliable and long-term access of poor households from peripheral urban zones to drinking water. Blary (1995) underlines that, to date, no study has compared the approaches of the various stakeholders of the most underserviced neighbourhoods. However, the scope and complexity of these problems call for innovative solutions in order to identify conditions favourable for the emergence of partnerships in a context of decentralization.

Theoretical framework and methodology

We applied the strategic analysis model of Crozier and Friedberg (1977) and the typology of Coston (1998) to specify the role of the actors and the different regulatory modes that the state can adopt in its relations with third-sector organizations.

The strategic analysis model

Strategic analysis is an organizational analysis model that aims to explain the relations between interdependent actors. Analysing the processes and functioning of partnership practices starting from the experience of the actors, it allows us to understand how different actors generate a collective action. Power concepts, uncertainty zones, and concrete action systems allow us to appreciate the motivations of the actors, the resources they have access to, the strategies and alliances that develop between them, the constraints to which they are subjected, and their limitations with regard to surrounding constraints. However, given that our study is about public actors and the informal operator cooperatives, the system we explored is characterized by non-precise boundaries where the actors' level of interdependence is weak.

The typology of Coston and state regulatory modes

It is important to shed light on the degree of institutionalization of third-sector initiatives with regard to the position of the state. The state can adopt three types of regulatory modes in its relations with third-sector organizations (Favreau and Hurtubise, 1993; Groulx, 1993; Lévesque and Mendel, 1999; Favreau and Vaillancourt, 2000; Vaillancourt et al., 2000). In the state-societal model, a predominant place is accorded to the state in the planning, organization, and provision of social services. In the neoliberal model, the market serves as the exclusive regulatory body as well as a mechanism to satisfy needs. Lastly, in the socio-community model, the state promotes a partnership-based relationship in which the culture and point of view of third-sector organizations are taken into consideration and influence government decisions. In this case, the state is a partner and regulator. These three models are ideal models in the Weberian sense. Moreover, the relationship model characterizing the collaboration between the state and the third sector should be a compromise between the state-societal model and the socio-community model. As observed by Coston (1998), the relations between the state and community organizations take diverse forms. Coston identifies eight types of possible relations between the state and NGOs: repression, rivalry, competition, contractual type, third party, cooperation, complementarity, and collaboration (Figure 7.1 and Box 7.1).

The typology of Coston is based on the analysis of three main parameters: opening of the state to institutional pluralism, formalism of the relations, and relations of power.

Methodological approach

For our case study, we chose to focus on Kisenso, one of the 24 communes of Kinshasa. Primarily an informal habitat, this zone of 17 neighbourhoods has nearly 270,000 inhabitants and a population density of 15,000 inhabitants

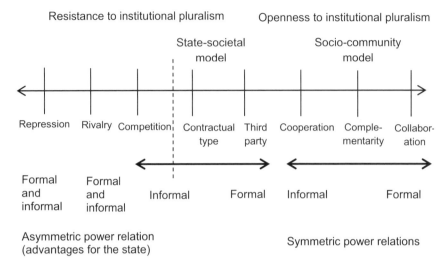

Figure 7.1 Typology of state/third-sector relations of Coston

Source: Coston (1998), revised and modified by Proulx et al. (2005)

Box 7.1 Description of Coston's typology

1 Repression: Strong resistance from the state to institutional pluralism; outright prohibition of third-sector organizations or of the exercise of some of their activities.

2 Rivalry: Strong resistance of the state to institutional pluralism through a restriction of permitted activities, very strict state control, and a refusal to provide any form of support to the third sector.

3 Competition: Resistance of the state to institutional pluralism. However, this resistance is less the result of a policy established to this effect than of a situation in which the state and third-sector organizations are in competition in the field, either politically, economically, or both: politically with regard to exercising activities pertaining to one and the same sector (exercise of local power); and economically with regard to obtaining resources from the community or, in the case of NGOs, foreign funds.

4 Contractual: The state maintains responsibility for the planning and organization of the actions and delegates operational activities to third-sector organizations to provide services. The opening to institutional pluralism, the intensity of inter-organizational relations, and the

symmetry of power relations are weak, while the formalism of the relations is high. The division of labour is based on comparative advantages and boundaries are blurred with regard to the sharing of responsibilities.

5   Third party: This type presents nearly the same aspects as the contractual type, such as a weak institutional opening, intensity of relations, and a symmetry of power relations. This type of relation also marks a division of labour between the state and the third sector, although the state and third-party subcontractors do manage financing and public authority together. The state determines the priorities and provides the funds, while the NGOs organize the production of services. However, the degree of formalism is weak.

6   Cooperation: The sharing of information is at the centre of the relationship. The opening to institutional pluralism, the intensity of the interorganizational relations, the degree of formalism of the relations, and the symmetry of the power relations are moderate. The community organizations perform their activities with respect to the regulations established by the state. Relations are limited to a non-constraining coexistence that can lead to duplications in the service offer. The state is sympathetic to the activities of the community organizations, without, however, being proactive in their support.

7   Complementarity: The role of the state and its establishments as well as the autonomy of the community organizations are recognized. There is information and resource sharing with the goal of reaching common objectives. The opening to institutional pluralism, the intensity of the relations, the degree of formalism of the relations, and the symmetry of the power relations are high. The complementarity can take place with regard to expertise and/or at the geographical level. The state may have the professional expertise, while the community organizations may have the social expertise and sometimes certain specializations in the service offer. The third sector may intervene in the regions where the state is absent.

8   Collaboration: The degrees of intensity and formalization of the relations are high. The third sector participates in the development of policies. The partners develop and co-produce services while maintaining their autonomy. The state accepts to share its responsibilities and operations with other actors. However, each actor maintains their respective autonomy, values, and mission. For Coston (1998), the relation of collaboration between the state and the third sector rarely becomes a true collaboration due to the difference of power that exists between the actors. It is almost impossible that power is actually shared fairly between the state and third-sector organizations due to the great disparities between the two actors with regard to size, resources, and other factors (Coston, 1998; Proulx et al., 2005).

per km^2. Erosive phenomena are found in three-quarters of its area (16.6 km^2). More than 60 per cent of the people in the zone are poor, 80 per cent are unemployed, and many of the youth are disaffected (CTB, 2004). We identi-fied three main partnerships in the zone: 1) partnership between public actors, informal operator collectives, one outside partner, and the users; 2) partner-ship between the Kisenso Health Zone, one international NGO, a cluster of local associations (water committees), and the users; and 3) partnership between the public utility, a local NGO, and the users.

Data collection For the data collection, we undertook documentary studies, ensured monitoring, and conducted semi-directed interviews. The interviews were started with a list of questions, following which the inter-viewees were given the opportunity to develop their answers and points of view. The interview guide was validated after a pretest was performed among the public actors and the managers of the community organizations involved in the provision of drinking water. We met with executives and agents of the public water distribution utility REGIDESO (Régie de distribution d'eau), government representatives (district mayor and some neighbourhood chiefs of Kisenso), managers of the Kisenso Health Zone, managers of community organizations, and delegates of a bilateral cooperation organization. In total, we realized 20 interviews.

Analysis and data processing

For each organization interviewed, we identified the following elements: partnership objectives, partnership process, actors' responsibilities and obli-gations, benefits, conflict management mechanisms, and partnership follow-up and evaluation. We then compared the content of these topics for each of the three main partnerships of our sample in order to be able to identify the similarities, differences, and possible relationships between them. For the interviews, we conducted a categorical type of content analysis that, devel-oped by L'Écuyer (1990) and Huberman and Miles (2003), was realized in four stages: 1) reading and recording of the interviews; 2) subdivision of the interviews into units of meaning based on a particular theme (determination of the statements); 3) codification and classification of the interviews (actors and partnership objectives, action process, participation in decision-making, sources of power, impact of the agreements, constraints, and perspectives); and 4) the analysis and interpretation of results. Moreover, we performed a vertical and horizontal analysis of the content. The vertical analysis consisted of considering the content of each organization in an independent manner, by comparing, for each category retained, the statements according to the groups of actors (public, community) and by analysing the nature of the part-nership. The horizontal analysis consisted of comparing the statements of the groups of actors for the three partnerships and of identifying the similarities and differences. As a last step, we interpreted the significance of the informa-tion gathered and prepared an explanatory summary statement.

Results

Provision of drinking water in the commune of Kisenso

In the urban and semi-urban areas of the Democratic Republic of Congo, drinking water supply is the responsibility of REGIDESO. In the commune of Kisenso, apart from this public utility, many stakeholders participate in the provision of drinking water, in particular the Kisenso Health Zone, the Church Saint-Étienne, the NGO CEMI (Centre Misericordia), and USADEK (Union des jeunes Sages de Kisenso). Despite their interventions, drinking water is accessible to only about 10 per cent of the entirety of the population (Zone de Santé de Kisenso, 2004) and some households continually use undeveloped sources of water.

A household spends on average $0.27 per day to access water, representing $8.10 per month. Almost half of the households in Kisenso have to spend 16 per cent of their income on water-related expenses. The price charged by the informal operator collectives is almost three times above the price offered by the public utility (Katsongo, 2006). Moreover, the average time per day spent obtaining water is estimated to be two hours, and can go beyond three hours in some neighbourhoods (Amba, Mbuku). The distance separating homes and water sources is 1 km or more.

Results of the three partnerships

In this section, we discuss the relationships established between public actors and informal operator collectives by describing three partnerships that existed with regard to the provision of drinking water to the population.

Partnership 1 – Partnership between public actors, informal operator collectives, one outside partner, and users The public actors are REGIDESO, the commune, and the neighbourhood chiefs. The role of REGIDESO is to bring its technical expertise to the informal operator collectives for the installation of the standpipe and the connection of the households to the public drinking water distribution network. The commune of Kisenso coordinates and supervises roundtables, while the chiefs of the 17 different neighbourhoods conduct public sessions concerning the choice of the water supply projects. The informal operator collectives (Church Saint-Étienne, NGO CEMI, and USADEK) have the role of sensitizing the users to well-founded partnership projects and to solicit their contribution in labour. They also prepare projects to submit to the consultation committees, ensure the realization of projects, and ensure the management of the sources of drinking water. The outside partner – Coopération Technique Belge (CTB) – plays the role of facilitator in the establishment of the links between the public actors and the informal operator collectives and finances the projects. Lastly, the users (inhabitants of the Mission, Kumbu, Mujinga, Bikanga, Kabila, and Libération neighbourhoods) provide the labour and offer their land for the set-up of the works.

Concerning the structure and mechanisms of collaboration, roundtables are held on an ongoing basis to select water supply projects (Comité local de développement, CLD, and Commission communale de développement, CCD). One respondent explained the role of the CLD as follows:

> At the level of each neighbourhood, the CLD examines the validity of the projects and their impact on the improvement of the living conditions of the inhabitants of the milieu. The neighbourhood chief serves as president of the CLD, but can also participate without being a member. After approval of the project at the neighbourhood level, the neighbourhood committee transfers the file to the CCD, which re-examines all projects of the commune of Kisenso, neighbourhood by neighbourhood, and transmits the selected files to the CTB.

The composition of the CLD is diverse, including church representatives, market gardeners, youth, NGOs, community networks, and neighbourhood chiefs, and delegates are selected by vote. The CCD, headed by the town magistrate, pursues almost the same objectives as the CLD, with the difference that it decides on projects that have already received approval from the respective neighbourhoods. The CCD has a consulting role, and it is the NGO or the association that signs the partnership with CTB.

Partnership 2 – Partnership between the Kisenso Health Zone, a cluster of local associations, an international NGO, and the users The Kisenso Health Zone (a division of the Department of Public Health) supervises the activities of the water committees in the management of the standpipes and ensures the follow-up and longevity of developed water sources. The informal operator collectives, represented by a cluster of local associations, ensure the daily management of the water supply points (finances, maintenance, service). As for the international NGO (OXFAM Great Britain), a respondent explained the organization's mandate as follows: 'OXFAM gave the money and provided the technical expertise. The members of the water committees and our team were trained by OXFAM to manage the standpipes (maintenance, accounting)'.

Lastly, the users (inhabitants of the Kisenso-Gare and Kabila neighbourhoods) provided the labour for the implementation of the infrastructures and some offered their land to allow for the installation of the standpipes or the development of the water supply sources.

With the aim of facilitating the consultation between the stakeholders, water committees were implemented by the local associations. Every three months, the representatives of the Health Zone, the delegates of the committees, and user representatives participate in meetings to evaluate the condition of the infrastructures and the financial statements of the committees.

Partnership 3 – Partnership between a public utility, a local NGO, and the users The local agency of a public utility (in charge of Kisenso) ensures the connection of the households to the public drinking water distribution network, operates the network, installs the piping system, and bills the users.

A local NGO (the Centre communautaire de développement humain – CCDH-12) has the mandate to facilitate relations between the public utility and the users, to enlist users in mobilizing funds for equipment purchases, and to encourage users to register with the public utility. The users (inhabitants of the Amba neighbourhood) pay contributions for the purchase of the equipment and supply labour during the works.

Here as well, a water committee was set up to facilitate consultation between stakeholders. It is composed of representatives of the users and the local NGO. This committee is mandated to organize the connections, discuss costs, and ensure the follow-up of the works. The committee members meet every six months to take stock of the works, discuss difficulties, and look for adapted solutions.

Comparative analysis

The comparative analysis was based on the following parameters: the formalization of the collaboration, participation in decision-making, access to and sharing of information, resource complementarity, capacity to mobilize financial resources, and the impacts of the agreements.

Formalization of the collaboration

In the first partnership, no formal agreement exists between the public actors and the informal operator collectives. However, a memorandum of understanding was concluded between REGIDESO and CTB to allow the operators of informal collectives to engage in the provision of drinking water in the poor neighbourhoods. The memorandum serves as a framework of dialogue and collaboration; however, because official collaborations are not yet authorized under current law, it remains informal. The first provision of the memorandum of understanding stipulates:

> While waiting for the adoption of an adapted institutional and regulatory framework that defines the roles and responsibilities of the different actors, the management structures of these, and the regulatory mechanisms, it is recommendable to establish a framework of dialogue and collaboration between REGIDESO and CTB concerning the different levels of responsibility in the management and implementation of the drinking-water supply projects, in particular with regard to the creation of autonomous mini-networks allowing for community management in peri-urban zones that have no connection to the water distribution networks of REGIDESO.

In the second and third partnership, the relations were formalized by the signing of a collaboration agreement that determines the roles and responsibilities of each actor.

Participation in decision-making

In the first partnership, the public actors and informal operator collectives have only a consulting role in the projects, with the final decision lying with the CTB. In the second partnership, delegates of the Health Zone and local associations participate in the water committee prior to any decision-making. In the third partnership, the representatives of the users and the local NGOs as well as a delegate of the local public agency consult and seek consensus prior to project launch and during project realization and follow-up. The local water committee formulates suggestions to the local public agency for improving the connections of the households to the public network.

Information access and information sharing

In all three partnerships, personal contacts are the main sources of information. In the first partnership, networks constitute an excellent means of exchange of information between the local NGOs. Moreover, announcements are posted at each neighbourhood office and a newsletter – the journal *Nzela ya Lobi* (meaning 'tomorrow's path') – is published monthly. In the second partnership, announcements are also posted in the health centres of each neighbourhood and at the office of the Health Zone. The community networks, composed mainly of women, play an essential role in the transmission of information between the Health Zone and the members of the water committees. In all three cases, there is no formal mechanism for sharing information and it is rare that the public actors respond to the messages transmitted by the informal operator collectives.

Complementarity and mobilization of resources

In all three partnerships, the data from the interviews show that the resources used for the implementation of common projects complement each other. For example, concerning the first partnership, a respondent explained 'The CTB uses the services of SNHR and REGIDESO, who provide experts for works concerning the provision of drinking water. These businesses provide technical expertise and training to local community organizations'.

As for the capacity to mobilize financial resources, no subsidy was granted by the state for the development of informal activities for any of the partnerships. However, in the third partnership, agents who realize works in the field are employed by the public utility and are, as such, remunerated by the state. In the first and the second partnerships, project financing is provided by the organization that is responsible for the financing and sale of the drinking water. The financial profitability of the micro-businesses is variable. In the first partnership, respondents underlined that the financial resources obtained were very good; and in the second partnership, that the non-payment of water had a big impact on the profitability of the water supply points. In the third partnership, the financial profitability depended more on the fees charged to the households. Irregularity in drinking water supply was found to de-motivate certain users, who then turned to independent suppliers.

Spin-offs of the partnership practices

There is still no veritable coordinating structure within the partnership, according to the respondents. Moreover, no cluster of informal operator collectives has taken shape. In the second partnership, the public and informal actors are represented within the collaborative structure and participate in decision-making, while in the first and third partnerships, the informal operator collectives have a consultation role only.

These partnership practices have led to the emergence of new modes of collaboration. In the first partnership, permanent consultation structures (CLD and CCD) emerged, while in the second partnership, local water committees constitute a permanent consultation framework. The second and third partnerships show signs of a decentralization of water management; however, this has remained largely informal and is practised largely without the signing of contractual agreements. In the second partnership, thanks to the partnership practices, the public actors and informal operator collectives were able to develop and improve their competencies and to access external financial resources (OXFAM). In the first partnership, CTB also played an essential role in the mobilization of financial resources.

The conclusion of partnership agreements allowed for the creation of jobs and implementation of new facilities and infrastructures, as explained by a respondent with regard to the first partnership: 'Thanks to the partnership, we have increased the production capacity and expanded our network. We now have 10 points of sale (six in the Kumbu neighbourhoods, two in the Amba neighbourhood, and two in the Mission neighbourhood)'.

The partnership practices, implemented since 2001, have also allowed the water needs of one portion of the households to be met. In fact, an evaluation study realized by CTB in 2006 with the support of COPEMECO (a Congolese confederation assisting small and medium businesses) and INADES reveals that access to drinking water is no longer a priority need. It ranks sixth among all other priorities in the neighbourhoods that have benefited from actions realized in partnership in the framework of the second partnership (Kisenso-Gare and Kabila). According to the results of an epidemiological survey conducted by the Kisenso Health Zone (Zone de Santé de Kisenso, 2004), the rate of waterborne diseases has dropped since the installation of standpipes. For example, in the Kisenso-Gare neighbourhood, the number of cases of waterborne diseases at the health centre dropped from 1,363 in 2003 to 1,283 in 2006, representing a 6 per cent drop (Zone de Santé de Kisenso, 2007). By contrast, in the neighbourhoods that benefited from the actions realized in the first partnership (Mission, Kumbu, Mujinga), access to drinking water still ranked third in 2003 and fourth in 2006. In the Mission neighbourhood, for example, 616 cases of waterborne disease were recorded in 2003 and 617 in 2006. In the Amba neigh-bourhood, which was the focus of the third partnership, access to drinking water is still the first priority. Between 2003 and 2006, the number of cases of waterborne diseases recorded at the health centre rose from 735 to 1,075.

The second partnership appears to be the most efficient. The relations between the public actors and the informal operator collectives were formal-ized by the signing of an agreement that specified a clear distribution of roles and responsibilities in the realization of joint projects. Public actors and informal operator collectives alike are represented within the collabora-tive structure and participate in decision-making. The community network, comprised mainly of women, plays a primordial role in the consolidation of the relations between the Health Zone and the water committees. The partnership practices have allowed the public actors and the informal oper-ator collectives to improve their competencies. Access to drinking water is no longer a priority need and the occurrence of waterborne diseases is less frequent. Financial profitability is difficult to assess, especially since certain committees refuse to submit their financial statements to the Health Zone, furthermore suggesting that embezzlement took place. Moreover, the public actors and the informal operator collectives benefited from the financial resources and the expertise of the NGO. In reference to the Coston model, this second partnership can be associated with the contractual (state-soci-etal orientation) type, the first with the rivalry type, and the third with the competition type.

Factors influencing the partnership practices

We analysed the factors influencing the partnership practices between the public actors and the informal operator collectives concerning the provision of drinking water. Some of these factors impede the process, while others accelerate the process.

Structural difficulties   At present, the main structural difficulty is related to the legal vacuum concerning the installations realized in the framework of the collaboration, which generates great confusion as to the status and operation of the works. The lack of formalization of partnership relations constrains the development of the partnership. In that regard, one respondent underlined: 'In a peri-urban environment, efforts of the NGOs should be encouraged. However, there is no water code and no regulation that defines the roles and responsibilities of each partner. There is no law that determines partnership relations. The law is still in the drafting process and will be enacted soon to authorize community organizations to serve zones not serviced by REGIDESO'.

Other factors impeding partnership relations are: the lack of a definition of the scope of intervention of the informal operator collectives, the absence of a legal status of the structures created in the partnership context, and the absence of official recognition by other state services of the legality of actions performed by informal operator collectives.

Functional obstacles   The main functional obstacle to good partnership relations is a lack of qualified personnel within the community organizations and the limited competence of public-sector personnel, as expressed by two respondents: 'The problem of access to water in the poor neighbourhoods of the city of Kinshasa has to do with the collaboration with the community organizations. However, a problem exists with regard to the training and retraining of human resources of our agents to adapt these resources to current needs' and 'From a technical point of view, the level of the NGOs is very low. Some NGOs could be said to be doing do-it-yourself, makeshift work'.

Moreover, the flow of information between the public actors and the informal operator collectives is poor, with interpretations and biases from both sides provoking relational problems and malfunctions. The weak capacity to mobilize local financial resources, due in particular to the poverty of the members of the community organizations and the lack of financial support of the state, constitutes another obstacle. The informal operator collectives criticize the restrictive conditions, in particular the imposed delays, for accessing assistance from donor agencies. The extensive power of local authorities in partnership structures (CLD and CCD) during decision-making also constitutes an impediment to the development of the partnership. Lastly, certain socio-cultural factors (tribalism, customs, beliefs, religion) inhibit the good functioning of the partnership.

Success factors

The public actors and the informal operator collectives mention as success factors the formalization of the collaboration, the decentralization of water services, capacity building, the implementation of a coordinating structure, the cluster of informal operator collectives, and the creation of a journal to disseminate information about water. The informal operator collectives hope for an improvement of the conditions for accessing outside financial aid and advocate the adoption of a business approach for the management of drinking water in order to ensure the financial viability of local water committees.

Discussion

The quality of drinking water supply in poor urban settings relies mainly on two factors: the decentralization of water services and the institutionalization of the collaboration between public actors and informal operator collectives. From a sustainable development perspective, the Declaration of Dublin (1992) on water insists, for one, on the need for the active and democratic participation of the community in the search for solutions to water problems at the local scale, and second, that decision-makers and populations should collaborate directly in the management of water services at this scale.

Decentralization of water services

Our research results show that the formal drinking water management system in Congo is strongly centralized. Although the municipality played an informal role in the first partnership, it was not even a part of the second and third partnerships. The current regulatory and administrative structures still do not endorse the establishment of true partnership relations. Sometimes there is a lack of collaboration between the different state services mandated with water, and regulatory mechanisms fail to efficiently target the most impoverished segments of the population.

The second partnership, which seems the most efficient, is of the contractual type and corresponds to the state-societal orientation. In this model, the state is considered to have the necessary resources to provide citizens with the goods and services necessary for their individual and collective development. However, the Republic of Congo is faced with too many financial difficulties to satisfy the population's need for drinking water. The law on decentralization in the Congo delegates certain responsibilities to the communes with regard to water management. However, this delegation of powers is not accompanied with the necessary financial resources, and human resources are limited.

The informal drinking water management system presently in place tends to weaken the municipality and is strongly dependent on outside aid. Not all neighbourhoods are served in the same way, and the price is three times higher than the one in effect in the public sector. Nor do all households have access to drinking water at all times. Water being an essential resource, the state should guarantee a minimum quantity of water to each individual to ensure their vital needs. For example, South Africa guarantees 25 litres per person and per day to each citizen (Faruqui, 2003). Another solution would consist of granting targeted subsidies to the poor populations.

Weaknesses of the institutionalization of the collaboration between public actors and informal operator collectives

The institutionalization of partnership relations between public actors and informal operator collectives is weak. Apart from professional support, no state subsidy was accorded to the development of activities of informal operator collectives. Assistance from outside partners was needed to implement the first and second partnerships. Local authorities, who are responsible for the longevity of the drinking water management system at their scale, do not have the financial and material resources necessary to ensure the long-term continuation of activities in the field. Gaps have also been observed at the level of technical and managerial skills, with both the public actors and the informal operator collectives.

The absence of democracy in the history of African societies and the low level of sophistication of their economies explain the weaknesses of the collaboration between state actors and civil society organizations. In fact, in

Sub-Saharan Africa, the imposition of a centralized nation state just after the independencies of the 1960s exacerbated the fragmentation of civil society. The existence of centralized and authoritarian regimes has persisted in a good number of countries. Since 1989/1990, political pluralism has slowly begun to be recognized in some African states and a democratic culture is slowly taking root. Civil society actors and structures have since tried to affirm themselves as representatives of the state. This context is important, as the existence of a solidarity-based socio-political environment largely influences the institution-alization of local partnerships (Geddes, 1998).

Moreover, certain members of the partnership structures who are public officials act indirectly as informal operator collectives. In the first partnership, for example, local authorities who manage the collaborative structures (CLD, CCD) with regard to the selection of projects agreed to commission certain projects to friends or family members, profiting from their strategic position and benefiting indirectly from the financing provided by CTB to informal operator collectives. For this reason, some officials may well have transformed themselves into representatives of civil society in order to receive outside financing. This leads to a strong overlap between the state apparatus and civil society, as corroborated by Chauvreau et al. (2001), who underline that certain officials hold several positions at the same time (in the state apparatus, in local power systems, and even in foreign aid projects), as well as by Peemans (1997) and Hibou (1999), who point to a lack of differentiation between the formal and the informal in Africa. On the one hand, the formal sector cannot circum-vent the illegal practices; on the other hand, the informal networks are very structured and hierarchized, and their social insertion is very pronounced. Moreover, family and ethnic links as well as tribalism play a major role in the functioning of the collaborative structures. In this sense, Peemans (1997) underlines that in the popular urban economy, family and ethnic links play an important role in the creation and functioning of small activities.

Conclusions

Our study shows that it was the second partnership, the contractual type, that was most conducive to collaboration between public actors and informal operator collectives in the provision of drinking water in the poor urban neighbourhood of Kinshasa, where our survey was conducted. The effective-ness of a partnership depends on the consultation between the partners, their capacity to mobilize financial resources, their links established with the outside environment, their capacity-building efforts, and the extent of their participation in decision-making, the last of which depends on the degree of formalization of the relations. However, at this stage it is difficult to establish whether the effectiveness of agreements is improving as relations become more formalized.

The current institutional context is not conducive to the emergence of a dynamic partnership, as a providentialist regulatory model is still in place. The structural, human, and institutional deficiencies observed are direct results of poverty affecting individuals and institutions. It is thus essential to integrate actions to a global strategy that fights poverty, to clarify the roles of each stakeholder, and to define new economic and institutional regulations within a framework of co-management or co-production of services. The following should also be promoted: the decentralization of water services, the development of a water code, the determination of performance indicators, the implementation of micro-credit systems, capacity building, and the guarantee of a minimum quantity of water to each individual.

We studied only three partnerships, which certainly do not represent all types of relations that the Congolese state and the informal operator collectives maintain. It would be interesting to analyse other sectors in which civil society organizations are active, in order to shed light on the relations between the state and informal operator collectives at a more comprehensive level. Future studies could also take into account the consequences of the democratization of the political system on the participation of informal operator collectives in the management of development projects at a local scale. For example, they could examine the perceptions of households of the way in which the partnership responded to their drinking water needs. The analysis of the impact of health factors on the reduction of the cases of waterborne diseases could also be further developed. Another future research topic could be to examine which coordination mechanism promotes the best pooling of interests between public and informal actors. Lastly, the level of the technical and managerial competencies of the local actors should be evaluated, together with an examination of how women, who are the most active members of the community network, could contribute to the consolidation of partnerships.

References

Blary, R. (1995) *Gestion des quartiers précaires: À la recherche d'alternatives d'aménagement pour les exclus de la ville*, Editions Economica, Paris.

Bonfiglioli, A. (2003) *Le pouvoir des pauvres. La gouvernance locale pour la réduction de la pauvreté*, United Nations Capital Development Fund, New York.

Chauvreau, J.-P., Le Pape, M., and Olivier de Sardan J.-P. (2001) 'La pluralité des normes et leurs dynamiques en Afrique. Implications pour les politiques publiques', in G. Winter (ed.) *Inégalités et politiques publiques en Afrique. Pluralité des normes et jeux d'acteurs*, pp. 146–62, Éditions Karthala and IRD, Paris.

Collignon, B. and Vezina, M. (2000) *Les opérateurs indépendants de l'approvisionnement en eau potable et de l'assainissement en milieu urbain africain*, World Bank WSP-AF, Washington DC.

Coston, J. M. (1998) 'A model and typology of government-NGO relationship', *Nonprofit and Voluntary Sector Quarterly* 27(3): 358–82.

Crozier, M. and Friedberg, E. (1977) *L'acteur et le système*, Éditions du Seuil, Paris.

CTB (Coopération Technique Belge) (2004) *La Coopération Technique Belge en République Démocratique du Congo*, CTB, Brussels.

CTB (2006) 'Rapport des ateliers d'identification des problèmes et priorisation des besoins dans la commune de Kisenso', CTB, Kinshasa.

Faruqui, N. (2003) 'Balancing between the eternal yesterday and the eternal tomorrow: Economy globalization, water and equity', in J. Rockstrom, C. Figueres, and C. C. Tortajada (eds) *Rethinking Water Management: Innovative Approaches to Contemporary Issues*, pp. 41–69, Earthscan, London.

Favreau, L. and Hurtubise, Y. (1993) *CLSC et communautés locales. La contribution de l'organisation communautaire*, Presses de l'Université du Quebec, Sainte-Foy.

Favreau, L. and Vaillancourt, Y. (2000) 'Le modèle québécois d'économie sociale et solidaire', *Les Cahiers du LAREPPS* (00-04, p. 27), Université du Québec à Montréal, Montreal.

Geddes, M. (1998) *Le partenariat local: une stratégie réussie pour la cohésion sociale?*, Eurofound, Dublin.

Groulx, L.-H. (1993) *Le travail social: analyse et évolution, débats et enjeux*, Éditions Agence d'ARC, Laval, QC.

Hibou, B. (1999) *La privatisation des États*, Éditions Karthala, Paris.

Huberman, M. and Miles, M. (2003) *Analyse des données qualitatives*, Éditions De Boeck Université, Paris.

Hugon, P. (2003) *Économie de l'Afrique*, Éditions La Découverte, Paris.

Kankwenda, M., Grégoire, L.-J., Legros, H., and Ouédraogo, H. (1999) *La lutte contre la pauvreté en Afrique subsaharienne*, Éditions Économica, Paris.

Katsongo, K. (2006) 'Accès à l'eau potable dans les quartiers pauvres de la ville de Kinshasa', *Bulletin de l'ANSD* 7: 11–42, Académie Nationale des Sciences du développement (R.D. Congo).

L'Écuyer, R. (1990) *Méthodologie de l'analyse développementale de contenu: méthode GPS et concept de soi*, Presses de l'Université du Quebec, Sillery, QC.

Lévesque, B. and Mendell, M. (1999) 'L'économie sociale au Quebec: éléments théoriques et empiriques pour le débat et la recherche', *Lien social et Politiques* 41: 105–19.

Maldonado, C., Badiane, C. and Miélot, A.-L. (2004) *Méthodes et instruments d'appui au secteur informel en Afrique francophone*, International Labour Organization, Geneva.

Peemans, J.-P. (1997) *Crise de la modernisation et pratiques populaires au Zaïre et en Afrique*, Éditions L'Harmattan, Paris.

Proulx, J., Bourque, D., and Savard, S. (2005) 'Les interfaces entre l'État et le tiers secteur au Quebec', *Les Cahiers du LAREPPS* 05-13, Université du Québec à Montréal, Montreal.

REGIDESO (Régie de distribution d'eau de la République Démocratique du Congo) (2001–2007), Annual report 2001–2007, REGIDESO, Kinshasa.

Sansom, K. (2006) 'Government engagement with non-state providers of water and sanitation services', *Public Administration and Development* 26(3): 207–17.

Sanyal, B. (1999) 'Potentiel et limites du développement "par le bas"', in J. Defourny, P. Develtere, and B. Fonteneau (eds) *L'économie sociale au Nord et au Sud*, pp. 179–94, Éditions De Boeck et Larcier, Paris and Brussels.

Stren, R. and White, R. (1993) *Villes africaines en crise. Gérer la croissance urbaine au Sud du Sahara. Côte d'ivoire-Kenya-Nigéria-Soudan-Sénégal-Tanzanie-Zaïre*, Éditions L'Harmattan, Paris.

UNDP (United Nations Development Programme) (2006) *Human Development Report*, UNDP, New York.

UN-Habitat (2005) *Financing Urban Shelter: Global Report on Human Settlements*, Earthscan, London.

Vachon, B. (1993) *Le développement local. Théorie et pratique. Réintroduire l'humain dans la logique du développement*, Éditions Gaëtan Morin, Boucherville, QC.

Vaillancourt, Y., Aubry, F., D'Amours, M., Jetté, C., Thériaut, L., and Tremblay, L. (2000) 'Économie sociale, santé et bien-être: la spécificité du modèle québécois au Canada', *Les Cahiers du LAREPPS* 00-01, Université du Québec à Montréal, Montreal.

WHO/UNICEF (World Health Organization and United Nations Children's Fund) (2000) *Rapport sur l'évaluation de la situation mondiale de l'approvisionnement en eau et de l'assainissement*, World Health Organization, Geneva.

World Bank (2003) *Private Participation in Infrastructure: Trends in Developing Countries in 1990–2001*, World Bank, Washington DC.

Zone de Santé de Kisenso (2004) 'Annual report', Zone de Santé de Kisenso, Kinshasa.

Zone de Santé de Kisenso (2007) 'Annual report', Zone de Santé de Kisenso, Kinshasa.

About the author

Kamathe Katsongo holds a master's degree in integrated development and management of forests and tropical land from ERAIFT (Université de Kinshasa), a master's degree in landscape planning and regional development from Université Laval, Canada, and a PhD in urban planning from the Université de Montréal, Canada. His research focuses on: urban planning and development policies; local environmental governance, water management, and anti-poverty strategies; the evaluation of environmental impacts; the management of resources and natural habitats (sustainable development); REDD (reducing emissions from deforestation and forest degradation) and climate change adaptation in the countries of the Congo Basin; and land tenure security in Africa.

Chapter 8

Rethink, reuse: Improving collective action capacity regarding solid waste management and income generation in Koh Kred, Thailand

Diana Guerra

Abstract

This action-research project – the Rethink Reuse Project (RRP) – taught vulnerable women and girls to become financially autonomous by reusing waste to create new products, and in so doing becoming environmental ambassadors. The project was carried out in Bangkok, Thailand, in the Kredtrakarn Protection and Occupational Development Centre, a shelter for women and girls from throughout Southeast Asia who are victims of human trafficking or other types of social abuse. Action research and product development methodologies were linked to create a successful programme in which women can explore waste reuse and develop means of coping with poverty and increasing self-esteem. The overall objective was to introduce environmental awareness into Kredtrakarn Home, including its surrounding community, and to provide participants with the skills, tools, and information necessary to maintain a long-term programme that integrates income-generating waste-reuse activities into their everyday lives.

Introduction

At a time when rapid economic development has created dynamism and wealth in Southeast Asia, the region has become dirtier, less ecologically diverse, and more environmentally vulnerable, as is confirmed by many environmental reports (ASEAN, 2002, 2006; UNEP, 2001, 2002; UNESCAP, 2006). Southeast Asia's environmental problems are also particularly complex and challenging in that they cannot be solved by any one country on its own (Litta, 2009).

While environmental awareness has increased in the region, the concept of sustainable development is still relatively new (UNESCAP, 2000). Because the root causes of environmental degradation are directly related to poverty, lasting solutions could be achieved by dealing with environmental and poverty issues in an integrated manner. Therefore, to break the vicious cycle of poverty and environmental degradation, efforts must be shifted from simply 'caring for the environment' to 'sharing for the environment', as declared at the Rio Summit in 1992.

Kredtrakarn Protection and Occupational Development Centre, commonly known as Kredtrakarn Home,[1] provides shelter to approximately 500 women and girls from throughout Southeast Asia who are victims of human trafficking or other types of social abuse. Established by Thailand's Department of Public Welfare in 1960, the home's mandate is to provide protection and assistance to women and girls through occupational development, psychosocial rehabilitation, and medical treatment. At least 1,000 women and girls go through the shelter every year, staying between several months to many years, depending on their legal situation. As the largest shelter in the country for human trafficking victims, Kredtrakarn Home plays an important role in the local community as well as the national context.

Because of its location on Koh Kred Island in the Chao Phraya River north of Bangkok, Kredtrakarn Home faces major challenges with regard to providing solid waste management. Despite efforts to collect all waste and to transport it from the island to the mainland by boat, a lot of waste floats all around the island. Although Thailand, including the island of Koh Kred, has a formal waste management programme, it has no formal recycling scheme (Angloinfo, 2011). The United Nations Environment Programme (UNEP, 2004b) states that most Southeast Asian countries generate huge volumes of formal and informal non-organic waste (manufactured materials) that are neither separated nor recycled.

The Rethink Reuse Project (RRP) is an innovative strategy that links action research to product design methodologies. The overall objective of this research and design project was to introduce environmental awareness into Kredtrakarn Home, including its surrounding community, and to provide participants with the skills, tools, and information necessary to maintain a long-term programme that integrates income-generating waste-reuse activities into their everyday lives, thereby improving their local environment.

Research questions: RRP

The aims of RRP were to evaluate the extent to which collective-action waste-reuse activities can contribute to local waste management; what role solid waste management and income generation can play in extending opportunities for Kredtrakarn students and local communities; and the extent to which reused waste materials can be incorporated into traditional craft techniques to develop products in a way that protects the environment and reduces poverty.

The main goal of the project was to implement FEM's International's Basic Business Program in Kredtrakarn Home and Koh Kred Island's local communities, in order to introduce an entirely new environmentally and socially responsible vision that builds self-esteem, relieves poverty, and promotes local solid waste management by generating income through creative waste reuse. At Kredtrakarn Home, women and girls earn an income from the products they produce during the occupational activities. The nine-month programme encouraged participants to improve their self-esteem and personal skills with the aim that, once outside the shelter, they could generate their personal income by transforming waste into raw materials. RRP showed that it is in fact possible to tackle poverty and local solid waste management issues simultaneously. RRP participants discovered the income-generation potential of waste reuse through the creation of reuse waste products. Every participant experimented personally with the process of cleaning, preparing, and reusing waste to create marketable products.

Literature review

Solid waste management is now a global issue (Bulle, 1999). Many different actors have experimented with various technological options to find viable ways of collecting and disposing of waste. These experiments have proven that solid waste management is more than just a technical matter (Dalla Torre, 1992) and must consider socio-political and cultural aspects, and seek solutions based on innovative policies, administrative restructuring, institutional and organizational agreements, as well as an informed public (Richardson, 2003). The conventional view is that it is best to leave waste management in the hands of the private sector or state programmes (Kant and Berry, 2001). However, the reality is that local companies and governments are generally not able or willing to manage these systems, due to a lack of financial, technical, and human resources. Despite these deficiencies, there are some examples of successful community-based systems from around the world (Ostrom, 1990).

The need to understand community participation and community-based environmental management initiatives has been addressed by researchers and concerned institutions for several years now. Authors, researchers, and development practitioners have been trying to change the traditional mindset that poverty is the cause of environmental deterioration and that the urban poor generate waste that degrades their habitat (Lee, 1994). Instead, the more common view now is that the urban poor are the victims rather than the cause of environmental deterioration. The premise is that, if given access to important resources such as land and support from external groups and institutions, low-income communities can improve and maintain a decent and liveable environment.

Lee (1994) suggests that support from external NGOs can be a powerful catalyst in assisting low-income communities in terms of empowerment and improving environmental conditions. She also states that the increasing activism of indigenous NGOs in mobilizing collective community efforts represents, for the longer term, a significant source of external support. Douglas et al. (1994) argue that the facilitation and implementation of such community-based efforts as empowering strategies for the poor and for improving their access to important environmental resources, particularly land, infrastructure, and services, is necessary for environmental management.

Klundert and Lardinois (1995) argue that a top-down approach to community development is neither effective nor sustainable. They state that intervention agencies, even with the best intentions, cannot impose 'foreign' concepts and programmes onto communities and expect positive and sustainable results. Instead, they argue that forging partnerships between communities and the private or public sector, both formal and informal, can be a successful approach to strengthening urban environmental management. Anschutz (1996) suggests that community-based waste projects often fail because households, not experiencing solid waste management as a concrete, pressing need, tend to be reluctant to participate in and pay for such services. Mockler's (1998) study suggests that a 'felt need' is a necessary prerequisite for the successful implementation of a community-based solid waste management system.

Within the scope of this chapter, we present the most common challenges of community-based solid waste management. Based on our literature review, no formal research has been done on the many existing projects that link income generation, waste-reuse activities, and social global issues.

Action research linked to a product design methodology for reuse materials

RRP was conceived through an original approach combining two methodologies: action research and product design (Table 8.1). The action-research methodology is based on a cyclical process in which research, action, and evaluation are interlinked. The design methodology, for its part, is based on a result-driven[2] view that seeks to solve solid waste management issues with creative means. The researcher combined these two methodologies following the steps in Table 8.1 in a parallel manner.

The project took place over a nine-month period, which was three months longer than anticipated in the initial project proposal. More time proved to be necessary to assess roadblocks for the adoption of the reuse concept and to create processes that could make RRP sustainable.

RRP goals related to outcomes

In the following, each of the project goals and outcomes is presented to facilitate an understanding of the overall project result.

> *Goal 1: Use the 'our waste is our resources' concept as a tool to share basic environmental consciousness skills.*

> *Outcome*: Creation of a long-term activity allowing reflection on, discovery of, and participation in the workforce on the basis of the reuse concept.

Table 8.1 Action-research methodology and product-design methodology in parallel

Action-research methodology	Product-design methodology (Design Council, 2011)
1 **Plan:** Evaluate local conditions and potential participants' receptiveness; assess local-community and target-group skills; select potential participant and community groups.	**Discover:** Begin with an initial idea or inspiration sourced from a discovery phase in which user needs are identified by either market research or user research.
2 **Observe:** Work in collaboration with FEM International director Lis Ensink-Suarez Visbal to launch the programme; customize the project to local conditions.	**Define:** Interpret and align the needs to business objectives that need to be achieved. Key activities during the Define stage are project development and project management.
3 **Act:** Link the action-research goals and design components to daily activities; demystify the business process and present it at an approachable level to different communities by applying it in a bottom–top way.	**Develop:** Period where design-led solutions are developed, iterated, and tested. Key activities and objectives during the Develop stage are multi-disciplinary working, visual management, and testing.
4 **Reflect:** To what extent has the project evolved? What new partners or stakeholders are involved in the project?	**Deliver:** Period where the resulting product or service is finalized and launched in the relevant market. Key activities and objectives during this stage are: final testing, approval and launch, targets, evaluation, and feedback loops.

For nine months, our main activity was to discover and put into practice all kinds of waste-reuse techniques with locally available materials. As a starting point, a basic waste-separation system was developed in which students were introduced to waste management. Students observed the quantities of waste produced and realized that plastic bags and plastic packaging were the most common materials. Reusing local waste was important for gaining credibility with regard to our claim that the potential to reuse materials is endless. Since plastic bags were the most common material, a plastic fusion technique was introduced involving the use of simple materials such as an iron and waxed paper. The technique consists of placing plastic bags between two sheets of waxed paper and passing a hot iron over them. The result – fused plastic bags – is a flexible material that can serve as raw material for multiple uses, such as aprons, curtains, or raincoats. During the entire programme, participants went through the creative process of reusing waste by experimenting with all kinds of materials. Participants applied traditional techniques for waste reuse and learned to develop added value products.

Goal 2: Develop reused waste products with locally available materials and traditional techniques.

Outcome: Product development and expansion of traditional handcrafted techniques through the reuse of materials coming from industrial and household waste.

Initially, women's accessories were created to motivate participants to discover the potential of the reuse concept. Within the programme, many reuse techniques were tested depending on the participants' interests. In Kredtrakarn Home, we experimented with several materials, including plastic bottles, plastic bags, and fabric waste from the textile industry. This was done in collaboration with the Home's four occupational sections plastic weaving, sewing, batik, and handicrafts.

Students already possessed various handicrafts techniques, especially crocheting, weaving, and sewing. Mixed technique samples were developed to make use of already existing products such as crochet flowers. In the home's plastic weaving section, plastic waste was transformed into a different plastic material, which was then used to create notebooks. The use of alternative materials such as plastic bottles was developed to create baskets and decorative accessories. Each woman and girl developed her own plastic bag material and created her own personal plastic bag product as handbags.

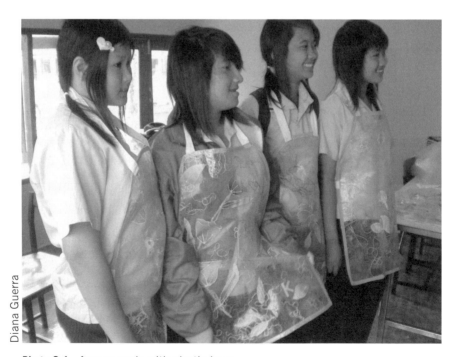

Diana Guerra

Photo 8.1 Aprons made with plastic bags

Photo 8.2 Plastic bag weaving with traditional techniques

Goal 3: Expand the basic business programme with environmentally related and creative activities.

Outcome: The basic business programme taught to more than 500 participants in a nine-month period.

The initial goal of the RRP was to reach as many participants as possible from the local community and Kredtrakarn Home. In Kredtrakarn Home, RRP reached more than 400 young women and girls, aged nine years and older, who were victims of either human trafficking or social abuse. A total of 40 members of the shelter's staff, including social workers, psychologists, and teachers, were introduced to basic business and social entrepreneurship methods using the 'our waste is our resources' concept. In the local community, RRP worked with more than 30 members of different community groups of Koh Kred Island, including the Koh Kred Muslim Women's Cooperative, the Koh Kred Adult Handicrafts Group, and the Pak Kred Adult School. The shelter's management also established a collaboration with the Ministry of Labour by developing a workshop for more than 100 people, both men and women, who were interested in learning innovative skills to create or improve their businesses. This workshop was very successful, with one trained participants going on to become a teacher of the plastic bag reuse technique for the Ministry of Labour in Bangkok.

Goal 4: Create a reuse section to figure as one of the main handicrafts activity sections and continue developing environmentally friendly and socially responsible products.

Outcome: Establishment of a fully equipped reuse section.

The reuse section was created with the Ecopolis project fund. A fully equipped workstation was established to allow for the long-term continuation of the reuse activities. A product label was developed, the 'Kiddi' product brand, under which all reused material products are now sold. Kiddi tags were developed to inform clients of the environmental importance of reusing waste. A product showroom and store was also set up in the shelter to present the reused waste products under the Kiddi brand.

Goal 5: Link income generation activities to local waste-management issues and empower local groups to spread the project.

Outcome: Fill the knowledge gap between environmental activities and social global issues such as human trafficking, thereby fostering the collaboration of institutions that normally have different responsibilities and mandates.

The initial goals were limited to the creation of a local supply network for obtaining ready-to-use waste materials for the products; establishing an outside partnership programme was thus not on the agenda. However, as time went by, the researcher realized that it would be very difficult to set up an in-house team that could run the reuse activities in a sustainable way. For example, it proved difficult to identify a leader who would appropriately champion the mission of the RRP project. Hence, a partnership was created with a reuse material laboratory called Scraplab from the Building Technology division of the Faculty of Architecture of Kasetsart University, a local design university. Headed by Prof. Dr Singh Intrachooto, a well-known designer in Thailand, Scraplab is a unique visionary project in which applied design research is used to empower the environmental efforts of industry by reusing waste to create products. This partnership was a key factor in consolidating the shelter's credibility towards RRP and developing a sense of ownership of RRP by local actors, who ensured the follow-up of the project. The Scraplab team, designer Jarupatcha Achavasmit, as well as Scraplab students empowered the project by creating innovative reuse ideas and techniques incorporating the shelter's know-how and machinery. Finding donations of industrial waste material was made possible through the university's network. Prof. Intrachooto and his team have a wide network of industries and businesses that are interested in donating their waste for socially responsible projects and Kasesart University design students support the reuse activities of Kredtrakarn Home. A long-term programme continues to exist with students assessing material donations for their suitability in RRP activities. The students also collaborate with staff from Kredtrakarn Home to teach the women and girls about product development and sales.

Achieved goals

Discovery of the therapeutic value of waste-reuse activities for vulnerable women

RRP made the researcher discover that waste reuse is not only an excellent tool to transfer environmental knowledge and create income, but, most importantly, to enhance the participants' emotional and psychological healing processes. During the project evolution, the researcher observed that the participants benefited from the reuse activities as a self-esteem-building experience. One teacher once said 'the women and girls appreciate the reuse activities a lot because they identify their lives with waste'. Turning waste into something useful resulted in a motivational activity for the participants. The activity demonstrated that it was possible to create something out of nothing, and this nothing reflects how they feel inside. Although this was not one of the expected outcomes, it provided RRP with further acceptance and credibility.

Transformation of a traditional business empowerment programme into a sustainable development empowerment programme

The RRP context was challenging because it required sophisticated non-verbal communication skills, as most participants spoke only their native language. Thanks to the researcher's methodology, a traditional business empowerment programme was transformed into a sustainable development empowerment programme. Applying income-generation tools and waste-management information, RRP introduced environmental concerns into a context where poverty alleviation, urban waste management, and self-esteem activities were needed in order to improve women's adaptive capacity to climate change.

Application of an innovative methodology to a change process

RRP was designed to tie in with all the already existing occupational activities at Kredtrakarn Home. However, its implementation required a certain shift in the mindset at the home to embrace the concept of turning waste into raw materials. Combining two methodologies, namely, action research and product design, gave the researcher a wide perspective for dealing with local resistance to change. The results-based method, according to which small steps can make big changes, combined with the cyclical process of action research in which research, action, and evaluation are interlinked, was a critical key to success in the intervention. Searching for outside partners was also crucial for the project's success since it promoted a better understanding of possible solutions for dealing with the local complexities of waste reuse.

Getting institutions with different mandates to collaborate in order to fill knowledge gaps between environmental activities and global social issues such as human trafficking

RRP fostered collaboration among institutions that normally have different responsibilities and mandates. For example, an academic institution, in this case Kasetsart University (Scraplab), seized the opportunity to link their environmental mission to a social purpose. The social purpose in this case was human trafficking: Thailand, along with the rest of Southeast Asia, is a global hub for human trafficking. According to the 2011 US Department of State Trafficking in Persons Report, more than 250,000 people, including children, are trafficked from, through, or to countries in Southeast Asia every year. Thanks to the collaboration, Prof. Intrachooto and his team are now aware of the possibility of expanding reuse activities at the country's nine permanent and over 70 temporary human-trafficking shelters.

Thanks to RRP, it was possible to successfully test how to fill the gap between environmental activities and global social issues such as human trafficking on the basis of a sustainable-development approach. RRP brought together stakeholders such as Koh Kred Island's community, including Kredtrakarn Home and Kasetsart University in Thailand. At Kredtrakarn Home, RRP participants make some income throughout their stay in the shelter, while being prepared at other levels to return to society as healthy and skilled as possible. To avoid participants being captured yet again by human-trafficking networks, women need to rebuild their self-esteem and become autonomous. Through the waste-reuse programme, women regained self-esteem by transforming 'something out of nothing'. Our project introduced the innovative approach of art therapy using waste reuse to cope with local needs of Kredtrakarn while linking these solutions to global environmental issues. For two years now, RRP has reached thousands of women, allowing them to discover their potential to become environmental ambassadors.

The creation of local ownership based on the criteria of international development agencies

Of the many international poverty-alleviation projects of international development agencies, not many are successful. One lesson learned from RRP is that in the Global South, success can be achieved by triggering events that change the availability of opportunities for people involved in development projects. Triggers, or triggering events, can be defined as circumstances that are catalysts for learning from existing conditions and for developing the capacity to change them. As noted previously, solid waste management calls for solutions that use imaginative policies, administrative reorientation, institutional and organizational arrangements, and an informed public (Richardson, 2003). Through RRP, the researcher explored the potential benefits of a creative approach by relating local waste-management issues to income generation and self-esteem-building activities for women and girls. RRP acted as a catalyst by empowering vulnerable women to become aware of global environmental issues and to become actively involved in waste management through waste-reuse income-generation activities. Prior to the implementation of RRP, local waste management was not seen as a 'felt need' at the Kredtrakarn Home. However, innovative poverty relief, income generation, and self-esteem activities are always needed in Kredtrakarn Home, given that the women and girls in the shelter have difficult social backgrounds. As Mockler's (1998) study suggests, 'felt need' is a necessary prerequisite for the successful implementation of a solid waste management system based on community and collective action. The RRP project was first rooted in a 'felt need for income generation' and then linked to the broader regional environmental issue of waste management.

Conclusions

Kredtrakarn Home serves as an example for many institutions in Thailand. The results of the RRP project helped to open the eyes of the Department of Social Development and Welfare to the myriad of possibilities for taking action regarding environmental issues. As our project shows, protection against human trafficking, occupational development, self-esteem building, environmental awareness, and income generation can be successfully linked in many ways. Future studies could complement this research by analysing similar case studies. In fact, some of the partners involved in this project have already expressed their desire to continue developing and expanding the reuse concept at the national level. RRP proved that it is possible to develop communities' capacities for coping with current global environmental challenges by fostering innovative activities. What started as a dream is now a success story, as demonstrated by the ongoing activities of the Reuse Centre at Kredtrakarn Home and its partnership with Scraplab. However, although reuse activities have become a part of the community's daily activities, there are still many challenges to overcome. Among these is the need to improve the quality of the products in order to successfully compete in ecologically responsible product niches, both domestically and abroad.

As Thailand's economy grows, environmental and human-trafficking problems continue to increase. However, RRP has planted a seed of hope by strengthening the belief that every single environmentally conscious action counts and can significantly and positively impact future generations.

Notes

1 See www.kredtrakarnhome.com/Eng/Event.htm
2 A management strategy focusing on performance and the achievement of outputs, outcomes, and impacts.

References

Angloinfo (2011) 'Recycling & renewable energy in Thailand', http://thailand. angloinfo.com/countries/thailand/recycle.asp [accessed 15 March 2011].

Anschutz, J. (1996) 'Community-based solid waste management and water supply projects: Problems and solutions compared: A survey of the literature', UWEP Working Document 2, UWEP, Nieuwehaven.

ASEAN (Association of Southeast Asian Nations) (2002) *ASEAN Report to the World Summit on Sustainable Development*, ASEAN, Jakarta.

ASEAN (2006) *Third ASEAN State of the Environment Report 2006*, ASEAN, Jakarta.

Bulle, S. (1999) 'Issues and results of community participation in urban environment: Comparative analysis of nine projects on waste management', UWEP Working Document 11, UWEP, Nieuwehaven.

Dalla Torre, C. (1992) 'Municipal solid waste management in developing countries: Problems and issues: Need for future research', No. 26, SANDEC publications, Switzerland.

Design Council (2011) 'The design process', www.designcouncil.org.uk/about-design/How-designers-work/The-design-process/ [accessed 15 March 2011].

Douglas, M., Lee, Y. S., and Lowry, K. (1994) 'Urban poverty and environmental management in Asia', *Asian Journal of Environmental Management* 2(1): 7–14.

Kant, S. and Berry, A. (2001) 'A theoretical model of optimal forest resource regimes', *Journal of Theoretical and Institutional Economics* 157: 331–5.

Klundert A. van de, and Lardinois, I. (1995) 'Community and private (formal and informal) sector involvement in municipal solid waste management in developing countries', Background paper for UMP, Gouda.

Lee, Y. S. (1994) 'Community-based urban environmental management: Local NGOs as catalysts', *Regional Development Dialogue* 15(2): 158–76.

Litta, H. (2009) 'Environmental challenges in South-East Asia: Why is there so little regional cooperation?', *Asian Journal of Public Affairs* 3(1): 76.

Mockler, M. (1998) 'Community-based solid waste management in Indonesia', background paper for World Bank, Jakarta.

Ostrom, E. (1990) *Governing the Commons: The Evolution of Institutions for Collective Action*, Cambridge University Press, Cambridge.

Richardson, D. (2003) *Community-Based Solid Waste Management Systems in Hanoi, Vietnam*, University of Toronto, Toronto.

UNEP (United Nations Environment Programme) (2001) *Asia-Pacific Environment Outlook 2*, UN Publishing, Bangkok.

UNEP (2002) *Global Environmental Outlook 3. Past, Present and Future Perspectives*, UNEP, Earthscan, London.

UNEP (2004a) *Environmental Indicators South-East Asia*, UNEP, Bangkok.

UNEP (2004b) *State of Waste Management in South-East Asia*, UNEP, Jakarta.

UNESCAP (United Nations Economic and Social Commission for Asia and the Pacific) (2000) *Urban Environment Management in Asia and the Pacific*, UN Publishing, Hangzhou, China.

UNESCAP (2006) *State of the Environment in Asia and the Pacific 2005. Economic Growth and Sustainability*, UN Publishing, Bangkok.

US Department of State (2011) *Trafficking in Persons Report*, US Department of State, Washington DC.

About the author

Diana Guerra is an independent environmental consultant specializing in solid waste and creativity. She holds a bachelor's degree in industrial design from the National Autonomous University of Mexico (UNAM) and a master's degree in environmental science from the Université du Québec à Montréal (UQÀM), Canada. She has worked as an environmental consultant for various private companies and NGOs in Asia, Latin America, and North America. In her work, Diana creates awareness for environmental issues using an innovative approach that combines creativity, income generation, and self-esteem development.

Chapter 9

Using participatory urban design to integrate organic solid waste management into urban agriculture: A case study from Cayagan de Oro City in the Philippines

Jeannette M. E. Tramhel

Abstract

For this action-research project, three communities in Cagayan de Oro City were engaged in a participatory design exercise to develop site plans for the integration of organic waste management into urban agriculture. The asset-based community development (ABCD) approach was used during community consultations as well as a five-day training course. These served both as a structured design 'charrette' and as a capacity-building exercise for a core group of 'Community EcoAids', who subsequently returned to their communities to spearhead the project's implementation. The project demonstrated that the ABCD approach is well-suited as a participatory urban design tool for the development of resilient and sustainable cities as it is consistent with the basic principles of urban design.

Introduction

As urban populations continue to grow throughout the world, so does the recognition of the environmental challenges facing such concentrations of populations and economies. Solutions to urban environmental problems require more than just changes to the built form. What is needed is a fresh look at how we design our systems when promoting sustainable urban living practices. More and more, engaging the community in the design of these systems is proving to be critical to their success.

This chapter describes an experimental participatory urban design project in Cagayan de Oro City, located in the southern Philippines, in which three communities developed their own plans for the integration of organic solid waste management (OSWM) into urban agriculture.

Context and relevance

Cagayan de Oro City was selected for this project for two reasons. One, it is home to the allotment garden concept introduced in 2003 by the Peri-Urban Vegetable Project (PUVeP) of Xavier University College of Agriculture. With the support of community groups and local government, the city today has 10 allotment gardens in operation for the benefit of the urban poor. Because PUVeP had also introduced composting, vermicomposting, and the use of 'ecosan' (ecological sanitation) urine diversion dehydration toilets, the gardening communities were already familiar with the benefits of using organic waste as fertilizer for food production (PUVeP, 2008).

The second reason for the choice of Cagayan de Oro City is the Ecological Solid Waste Management Act (RA, 9003) of the Philippines and a supporting municipal ordinance (no. 8975-2003) of Cagayan de Oro City. This legislation, which prescribes separation at source, recycling, and composting, represents an important shift in municipal planning, as it is a move away from the conventional single, centralized dumpsite towards a decentralized approach with several smaller facilities, referred to as materials recovery facilities. What emerged from discussions with Dr Robert J. Holmer, director of PUVeP, was the need to explore how the allotment garden concept could be adapted to meet this legislative requirement for decentralized OSWM.

After conducting background research (including review of maps, data and legislation, relevant literature, and precedent studies) and in consideration of the working knowledge already gained from local partners, steps were taken to develop an effective participatory process for accomplishing this task together with the community.

Literature review on the participatory process

Engaging 'beneficiaries' in participatory research has been a growing trend in development over the past two decades (Redwood, 2009). This includes participatory action research, most likely developed first by Chambers (1983), and, in the Philippine context, a process known as community organizing participatory research (Mindanao Training Resource Centre, 1992). Various names are used to describe such participatory practices; however, what they share is a recognition of the significant benefits that accrue from the internal community process and the notion that 'the only real lasting effect [from external research] is the community's capacity to organize' (Freedman, 1994: 57). Although participatory action research promotes a bottom-up, inside-outward approach to development, the process begins by identifying problems, usually by means of a SWOT analysis. Community organizers who use such methods commonly find that when participants begin the process by focusing on needs, they tend to look outward for solutions, and that it then becomes very difficult to turn that process around.

The asset-based community development approach, as developed by Kretzmann and McKnight (1993), resembles other participatory methods, however, with the difference that its process begins by focusing on community assets rather than needs. Thus, while this approach also takes a bottom-up, inside-outward approach, it begins with a recounting of community success stories, which then form the basis for identifying community assets.

Participatory urban design is rooted in a philosophy, also shared by participatory action research, that holds that 'the environment works better if the people affected by its changes are actively involved in its creation and management instead of being treated as passive consumers' (Sanoff, 2000: x). Moreover, urban design is inherently an asset-based approach, given that the designer is generally encouraged 'to begin with what is already there'. Because of the similarity of participatory urban design and participatory action research, the asset-based community development approach was considered to be well-suited for the participatory design process in this project.[1]

Approach

The commonly used tool in such a process is the design charrette,[2] which 'operates simultaneously as a product and a process' (Sanoff, 2000: 50). It usually takes the form of an open studio with a structured schedule, flexible opportunities for participation, and a design problem to be addressed over a three- to five-day period. The charrette can be used in a variety of situations, but must be adapted so that community participants are empowered with the motivation to create the best solution for themselves (Faga, 2006). Discussions with various sources in Cagayan de Oro suggested that it was not realistic to expect three to five days of participation from a representative demographic group that cuts across all sections of the community. This gave rise to the idea of restructuring the charrette into a five-day workshop that would simultaneously serve as a capacity-building course for community representatives. This course would be taken by teams of seven to eight members from each of the three *barangays* (villages) who expressed an interest in the topic and who had already demonstrated leadership potential.

The three *barangays* that were selected for the project – Lapasan, Kauswagan, and Macasandig – already had some familiarity with allotment gardens and had expressed interest in participating. The participatory process that was ultimately developed consisted of two half-day consultations in each *barangay*, a five-day Community EcoAid training course, and follow-up sessions in the communities with the assistance of EcoAids. The process, which enjoyed the support of the municipality and the three *barangay* councils, is described below.

Barangay *consultations*

Barangay consultations were facilitated in the local language by members of the Technical Working Group, consisting of a team of experts selected by the city administration from several of its departments. The consultations were intended to be fully inclusive, with representation from all kinds of stake-holders, including waste producers (e.g. households, businesses, and market vendors), waste pickers and collectors, potential end users (gardeners and commercial growers), local leaders, NGOs, and marginalized groups. However, participation had to be limited to 50 members from the community to keep the consultations manageable.

After introductions, participants were divided into small groups and encouraged to share their 'success stories' – namely, any accomplishment relating to OSWM or urban agriculture, be it large or small, achieved by members of the community, either together or individually. Among the stories shared were a clean-up drive for the drainage canal, a sign prohibiting informal dumping, and an existing composting operation. While a representative from each group recounted these stories to the plenary, participants identified the community assets (i.e. skills, people, and physical resources) that had been employed to achieve these results. Then everyone again gathered to locate these assets on a base map (Photo 9.1). Major sources of organic waste were identified with blue dots, and existing or potential sites for urban agriculture were indicated by green dots. This exercise encouraged a shift in the mindset among participants towards viewing organic waste as a community asset. These maps were also presented to the plenary and information from them was later consolidated. Participants were then invited to develop a vision statement for the integration of OSWM into urban agriculture in their community.

At the start of the second consultation, results from the first session were presented to participants for review and validation (namely, consolidated maps, vision statement, and inventory of community assets). In a brain-storming session, participants were then asked to come up with ideas for ways to integrate OSWM into urban agriculture, to write these ideas onto meta-cards, and to position these cards around the posted community vision state-ment. In a plenary, the group sorted through their ideas, linking them with the community assets that had been previously identified. Guided by the facilitator, the group discussed and prioritized these ideas and was then asked to select one idea as the basis for a pilot project to be developed further by the community representatives. Perhaps not surprisingly, in all three *baran-gays*, the selected idea in some way involved the establishment of a materials recovery facility and an allotment garden. Consultations concluded with the selection of seven to eight individuals who would attend the Community EcoAid training course and develop the project proposal. Others were asked to lend their support and return for follow-up discussions concerning the project implementation.

Community EcoAid training course

The course served two purposes: 1) as an alternative to the traditional design charrette, the EcoAid training course was a participatory design workshop allowing trainees to develop a site plan for their own communities over the

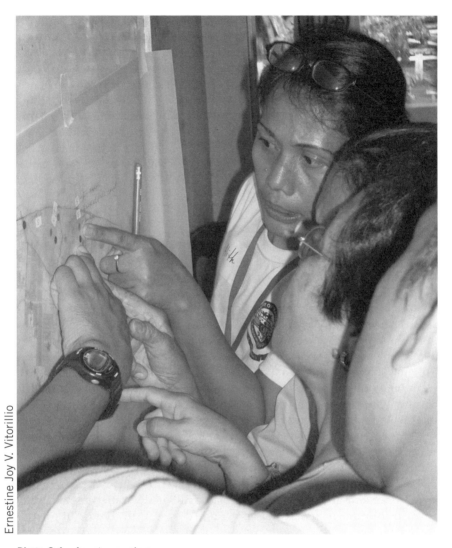

Ernestine Joy V. Vitorillio

Photo 9.1   Asset mapping

course of five days; and 2) it served as a capacity-building exercise to foster community-based environmental leadership. Prior to the course, a meeting was held with the trainees in their respective *barangay*, where they were instructed on how to conduct a visual inspection and documentation of the site that was selected for their pilot project. Applying the same approach used during the consultations, each team also developed a site-specific asset map, which served as the basis for subsequent course activities. This first exercise established an important link between the *barangay* consultations and the training course. In addition, it illustrated the parallels between asset mapping as part of asset-based community development and site analysis in participatory urban design.

One of the course objectives was to provide trainees with a basic understanding of the principles behind waste separation, the advantages of 'closing the nutrient loop', the basics of composting and its use in agriculture, and the socio-economic dimensions of waste management. The second objective was that, by using this information as a team to address a waste issue that the community had identified, the learning process would serve to solve actual problems rather than remaining an academic exercise. Third, it was hoped that by developing an actual site plan, the teams would find ways to actualize the visions developed by their respective communities during the consultations.

These objectives were achieved through a combination of lectures, hands-on exercises, and field trips. The course content covered the following topics: basics of separated solid waste management; benefits of the use of compost; basic principles and methods of composting/vermicomposting; underlying legislative requirements; challenges in waste management from the municipality's perspective; and health risks due to improper waste management. A session on city planning and urban design explained planning tools such as land use zoning as well as the principles of 'designing with nature' (McHarg, 1967) and creating 'continuous productive urban landscapes' (Viljoen, 2005). This introduced trainees to the challenges of shifting from conventional planning to the design of resilient urban systems. It also offered participants another perspective from which to consider their individual pilot projects, namely, the context of the broader urban setting.

Another session focused on how the commercial sector could be engaged. For example, given that compost and vermicompost are available for sale, the teams were asked to identify potential buyers in their communities and to develop a marketing strategy for the end products. The goal was to encourage creative thinking about waste as a misplaced resource and the reuse of locally generated organic material. This also required trainees to consider the socio-economic dimensions of solid waste management, such as the functions served by waste pickers and dealers. Rather than inducing a displacement of these people as a result of a change in solid waste management, the teams were encouraged to find ways to integrate these community members into their projects. Given that a successful implementation requires support from the broader community, the teams were also asked to develop materials for an information education campaign to encourage community engagement. To complete the course and receive certification, each trainee had to earn a pair of composting gloves by taking part in the barrel composting exercise (Photo 9.2). The information acquired through these activities was then applied in the development of the pilot projects.

Ernestine Joy V. Vitorillio

Photo 9.2   EcoAids – composting

Design principles and process

The guiding principle for these projects was environmental sustainability, given that the primary objective was a site plan for the integration of OSWM into urban agriculture to 'close the nutrient loop'. However, social and economic sustainability were also important considerations. For example, the projects were expected to build upon and strengthen existing social capital within the community (e.g. by integrating tricycle drivers as collectors) and the teams were supposed to consider ways to offset the cost of their operations (e.g. through market sales of compost and vermicompost).

The design process had started with *barangay* consultations, which resulted in a vision statement and community asset map for each *barangay*. It continued with the development of site analysis and base maps by the trainees. Various activities during the training course yielded results that were used to inform the design proposals. Each team was given a set of materials: base maps of the *barangay* and project site, asset maps prepared during the consultations, aerial photographs, and design materials (paper, markers, and transparencies). They also had computer access to satellite Photory and were able to consult with members of the Technical Working Group for assistance with technical questions (e.g. GIS data or information on composting and agricultural production).

Since most trainees did not have previous experience with site design, they were given a step-by-step explanation of the design process, together with a simple example and were offered guidance throughout the process. Each team developed its own design concept, which was then presented and discussed by the group as a whole. After incorporating this feedback, the teams further developed their design concepts into site plans and project proposals. Friendly rivalry between the three teams resulted in some good fun and tested the feasibility of their ideas.

Project outcomes

The outcomes of the project were:

1   Site plans and implementation proposals: at the end of the course, final presentations by each team were made to *barangay* officials and other invited guests. The site plans developed by the teams were both the outcome of the training course and the starting point for further project development and implementation.[3]

2   Community follow-up: after the training, each team made an official presentation of its proposed pilot project to their respective *barangay* councils. Follow-up consultations were then held with the community to provide an opportunity for feedback on the draft plans and to garner support for project implementation. The original plan of this project was, following approval of the plans by the community and the council, to move towards the implementation phase. However, this proved to be a challenge in all three *barangays*, as explained below.

3   Capacity building for environmental leadership: all trainees received certification as 'Community EcoAids'. The group composed of 23 EcoAids called itself MALAKAS (derived from 'MA' for Macasandig, 'LA' for Lapasan, and 'KAS' for Kauswagan), which also means 'strength' in Filipino. MALAKAS decided to meet quarterly, on a rotational basis in each of the three *barangays*, to provide a forum for discussion and to offer each other support during project implementation. In the months that followed, MALAKAS began by implementing elements of their project proposals. For this, they replicated training and exercises from the course for other community members and conducted house-to-house information education campaigns on waste separation and collection.

4   Follow-up visit 18 months later: approximately 18 months after the community consultations and the completion of the EcoAid training course, the researcher/author revisited the communities to evaluate any long-term impact of the project.

Project impacts

In Macasandig, the materials recovery facility site is now fully operational, with the active participation of at least two EcoAids and the support of the *barangay* council. The original building has been enlarged with a caretaker housing unit and the facilities have been expanded by two new buildings. Unsorted waste is now collected from households in the pilot area of the *barangay* and is brought to the site, where it is sorted. (The EcoAids had conducted door-to-door information education campaigns about waste separation. However, the current plan is to implement a separation-at-source regulation once the households are accustomed to regular collection.) The *barangay* council has implemented a household collection fee, the proceeds of which, together with the revenue received from the sale of recyclables, partially subsidize the collection costs.[4] Organic waste is now composted and used as a medium together with rice hulls to plant ginger cuttings. The first harvest of the crop is yet to be made; however, as ginger is a lucrative cash crop, it can be expected to help offset the cost of materials recovery facility operations.[5] As these continue to expand and more compost is produced, it is conceivable that it will be used by gardeners in the allotment garden that is directly adjacent to the facility. (At the time of the follow-up visit, the garden was still being rehabilitated after serious flood damage.) While it cannot be claimed that the project caused implementation of the materials recovery facility, it can be argued that it served as a catalyst in that regard.

In Lapasan, the *barangay* council has not been able to secure access to the site slated for the materials recovery facility and for which the EcoAids had developed a facility site plan. Subsequent to foreclosure proceedings, that vacant plot of land is now owned by the Philippine National Bank, and visits and letters to local and national bank officials (by the author, the director of PUVeP, *barangay* officials, and the local congressman) have not been met with any response. Moreover, the allotment garden on the site directly adjacent to the site slated for the facility has been closed. The landowner declined to renew the five-year term agreement with the *barangay* council, which had stipulated that the vacant lot could be used for local food production provided that no permanent structures would be erected. In the interim, another vacant lot has been brought into production as an allotment garden, but it is not well situated to serve the dual purpose of the *barangay*'s materials recovery facility. Despite these setbacks, the *barangay* council and the Lapasan EcoAids remain optimistic that a suitable site will be secured eventually. In the meantime, the *barangay* has received barrels for household waste collection that were donated by a local NGO, making it possible for the EcoAids to continue with their information education campaigns aimed at households to encourage separation at source. The *barangay* has also been given a biodigester that has yet to be installed and made operational. Here as well, the lack of an available site in this densely populated urban district is what limits implementation. However, on the whole, the related activities underway and the donations from the community suggest that something of value remained after the end of the project.

In Kauswagan, the situation is similar. The *barangay* council has not been able to secure an agreement with the landowner of the proposed site. As an interim measure, the council permitted the EcoAids to develop a 'mini facility' and a garden for demonstrative purposes at the premises of the *barangay* hall. The area showcases a small garden as well as composting and recycling bins. Here too, the EcoAids continue with an information education campaign and the council continues to seek out vacant land that could serve as a site for a materials recovery facility and allotment garden.

MALAKAS has continued with its quarterly meetings. A loosely formed steering committee on environmental planning has recently emerged, referred to as the 'MinUrbGroup'. The committee is spearheaded by leadership at Xavier University and has members from, among others, three other local universities and the City Planning Office. Three representatives from MALAKAS, one from each *barangay*, have been invited to sit on this group. Support for the ongoing activities of MALAKAS has been voiced by the City Planning Office.

The city council is considering a municipal ordinance wherein *barangays* that have implemented household waste collection programmes will be eligible to receive funds from the city budget to offset their collection costs, and which can be applied towards the securing of a site for materials recovery facilities. Again, this possibility cannot be claimed to be a direct result of the project; however, it is fair to say that the project may well have provided some impetus.

Project sustainability

The following project elements enhance the long-term sustainability of the projects:

- *Development of human resources* – a total of 23 individuals from the three participating *barangays* were trained as 'Community EcoAids'.[6] They gained useful knowledge and skills in the basics of OSWM and urban agriculture. This 'privilege' has elevated the status of these individuals within their communities and their commitment to follow through with the implementation. Their membership in MALAKAS, a group they themselves initiated, and its ongoing support should also help in this regard. By meeting on a rotational basis, the EcoAids follow the progress in each *barangay* and learn from each other.
- *Community involvement* – about 50 community members, representing the interests of various stakeholders, participated in each of the two consultations that took place in each of the three *barangays*, as well as in the follow-up activities conducted by the EcoAids after the training course. These members thus have an interest in the project's implementation.

Every attempt was made to include the voice of all stakeholders that could be affected by the project.

- *Official leadership* – the councils endorsed and offered support to the project in front of their communities and therefore have an interest in the implementation. The city government also offered its support, although this could change with a change in leadership.
- *Technical support* – the Technical Working Group, composed, among others, of representatives from the municipal government departments of waste management and agriculture, also have an interest in the successful implementation of the project that they were instrumental in developing.
- *Capacity building* – over the course of the project, a solid working relationship was developed between the Technical Working Group, the *barangay* councils, the EcoAids, and many others in the city. The creation of MALAKAS also strengthened linkages, mainly among the individual participants within each community, between the participants and their respective leaders, between the three MALAKAS communities, and between the leaders of those communities. The project has the support of Xavier University and the City Mayor's Office through the planning and development coordinator.
- *Legislative underpinnings* – the city council is presently considering an ordinance wherein those *barangays* that have implemented household waste collection programmes will be eligible to receive funds to offset their collection costs and that can be used towards the securing of a site for a materials recovery facility.

Further recommendations and research

To maintain the ongoing enthusiasm of MALAKAS, this group should be given financial support to cover their travel expenses, costs for their quarterly meetings, refresher training, and possibly for a website. MALAKAS could also be enlisted to assist with similar projects, such as the Clean Air Initiative for Smaller Cities.[7]

Though framed by an urban design perspective, this project was interdisciplinary in its approach and content. Thus, there are many aspects that could be enriched with further research. For example, the financial sustainability of the materials recovery facility operations could be investigated with appropriate cost–benefit analyses.

Project achievements

This project demonstrated, as other projects have, the value of community engagement in design processes. Although not an original concept in itself, the project was unique in that it applied the concept to the design of sustainable urban systems, where community leadership and user involvement are critical to successful implementation. By structuring the traditional design charrette as a training course, it was possible to achieve two complementary goals: participatory urban design and capacity building. The project also demonstrated the applicability of asset-based community development to participatory urban design for solving urban environmental problems.

A 40-minute documentary film was made about this project, describing the process that was used for the consultations and the site plan development. The documentary 'MALAKAS! Using Asset-Based Community Development in the Design of Sustainable Cities' can be viewed at www.youtube.com/user/IDRCCRDI#p/a/u/0/BEts_EhXPok

Notes

1   The asset-based community development process had been previously applied during the development of the allotment gardens, as described in Holmer and Mercado (2007).
2   A (design) charrette is a collaborative session in which a group of people work intensively with focused and sustained effort towards a solution to a design problem. Charrettes serve as a way of quickly generating a design solution while integrating the aptitudes and interests of a diverse group of people. In urban planning, the charrette has become a technique for consulting with all stakeholders and typically involves intense and possibly multi-day meetings with participation from municipal officials, developers, and residents (adapted from Wikipedia, http://en.wikipedia.org/wiki/Charrette [accessed 16 June 2010]).
3   This research is part of the author's master's degree in urban design. To fulfil certain degree requirements, the author chose the site plan that had been developed by one of the teams (Barangay Lapasan) and translated that team's design concept using conventional design language. The site plan was then further developed in subsequent design drawings.
4   The collection fee is PHP 10 (US$0.20) per month per household. Recycled metal can be sold for PHP 4.50 (US$0.10)/kg, plastic for PHD 16.0 (US$0.36)/kg, and cardboard for PHP 2.50 (US$0.05)/kg. The *barangay*'s revenue from sales of recyclables was PHP 11,000 (US$250.00) in two months.
5   The projected returns are 10 kg of ginger per sack, at PHP 60 (US$1.35)/kg, such that 100 sacks will generate PHP 60,000 (US$1,375).
6   Ideally these were to have been selected by their respective communities during the consultation process. Although their selection was invariably influenced, to a greater or lesser extent, by the local leadership in all three *barangays*, this did not turn out to be a problem as anticipated. All participants were motivated during the course and showed themselves to be active in their communities after the training.
7   Cagayan de Oro is one of the two cities in the Philippines that were selected to participate in the GTZ programme Clean Air Initiative for Smaller Cities in Southeast Asia.

References

Chambers, R. (1983) *Rural Development: Putting the Last First*, Longman, London.

Faga, B. (2006) *Designing Public Consensus: The Civic Theatre of Community Participation for Architects, Landscape Architects, Planners and Urban Designers*, John Wiley & Sons, Hoboken, NJ.

Freedman, J. (ed.) (1994) *Development from Within: Essays on Organizing Communities for Self-Sufficiency*, Institute of Primary Health Care, Davao Medical School Foundation, Davao, Philippines.

Holmer, R. J. and Mercado, A. B. (2007) 'Asset-based community development in urban agriculture: Experiences from the Southern Philippines', *UA Magazine* 18: 29.

Kretzmann, J. and McNight, J. (1993) *Building Communities from the Inside Out: A Path Towards Mobilizing a Community's Assets*, The Asset-Based Community Development Institute, Northwestern University, Evanston, IL.

McHarg, I. L. (1969) *Design with Nature*, The American Museum of Natural History, The Natural History Press, Garden City, New York.

Mindanao Training Resource Centre (1992) *Training Package on Community Organizing – Participatory Action Research*, Institute of Primary Health Care, Davao Medical School Foundation, Davao, Philippines.

PUVeP (Peri-Urban Vegetable Project) (2008) *Philippine Allotment Garden Manual with an Introduction to Ecological Sanitation*, Peri-Urban Vegetable Project, Xavier University College of Agriculture, Cagayan de Oro, Philippines.

Redwood, M. (ed.) (2009) *Agriculture in Urban Planning: Generating Livelihoods and Food Security*, Earthscan and International Development Research Centre, London and Sterling, VA.

Sanoff, H. (2000) *Community Participation Methods in Design and Planning*, John Wiley & Sons, Hoboken, NJ.

Viljoen, A. (ed.) (2005) *CPULS Continuous Productive Urban Landscapes: Designing Urban Agriculture for Sustainable Cities*, Architectural Press, Elsevier, Oxford.

About the author

Jeannette M. E. Tramhel works as a consultant at Plan:Net Limited, Calgary, and also runs her own consulting practice (www.foodjusticebydesign.com). She holds a bachelor's degree in agriculture from the University of Alberta, Canada, an LLB from Queen's University, Canada, an LLM (international law) from Georgetown University, USA, and a master's degree in environmental design from the University of Calgary, Canada. This academic background enables Jeannette to apply an interdisciplinary and systemic approach when working on the complex issues around food security, legal empowerment, and sustainable environmental planning.

Conclusion: The challenges of sustainable cities for research and practice

Mélanie Robertson

This book has highlighted a dynamic mix of academic research and design projects from fields such as architecture, environmental science, urban planning, and agroforestry. The studies presented in each chapter have developed relevant tools and methods for conducting interdisciplinary participatory research in cities. Moreover, the resulting data and interventions represent valuable bases from which to engage in a new generation of research on these topics. In fact, this is exactly what several of the authors plan to do.

By embracing multidisciplinary perspectives on urban life, the book attempts to go beyond the conventional 'siloed' research approach wherein the various disciplines fail to effectively communicate their findings or to build on the findings of other disciplines. The individual studies in this book draw theoretical and methodological insights from various fields to explore the complex relationships between humans – including the social, historical, psychological, and economic dimensions – and the natural and built environments. In doing so, they draw explicitly or implicitly on human-ecological principles, informed by a body of thought that views humans and human establishments as part of a natural ecosystem. In this regard, the studies of Pinard and Gagnon are exemplary. The premise of Pinard's study was that the women's compound is part of a natural ecosystem rather than simply a stage upon which human activity takes place. With this integrated approach, food security, health, and environmental and sanitary degradation were all treated as principal parameters in the design and construction of urban planning projects alongside the conventional economic or material constraints.

Similarly, Gagnon adopted an 'ecohealth' approach to explore how environmental contamination is mediated through social and cultural practices and the built environment. This approach was presented as a trans-disciplinary method that integrates the knowledge, experience, and concerns of researchers from different disciplines. Both Pinard and Gagnon, as well as Ndiaye, drew on economic, social, health, and environmental knowledge that had been generated during previous research projects of the IAGU on the impacts of the Mbeubeuss landfill, reflecting a valuable dialogue between researchers.

All the studies were based on the recognition that, given the complexity of human–environmental interactions, solutions to environmental problems cannot be merely technical and that, by consequence, interventions in the built environment cannot be divorced from social, cultural, and political concerns. As such, Lafontaine-Messier integrated technical insights from agronomy as well as social, economic, and political analyses into her project, which explored the implementation of fruit-producing trees in urban agro-eco systems. The study by Ejigu explored socio-spatial interactions – incorporating insights from geography, sociology, and architecture, and employing participatory ethnography as a research methodology. The study by Guerra explored waste management issues and combined insights from environmental science, design, business, culture, politics, and social psychology.

Aside from a rich interdisciplinary dialogue, the studies employed a variety of methodologies that built upon one another in an iterative manner. Researchers promoted and engaged in crossovers between action research, creation research, theoretical and applied research, and participatory approaches. As a result, their work was interactive rather than linear, with research, action, and creation nourishing each other reciprocally. The essential participatory and collaborative characteristic of these approaches consisted of the condition that the process be shared among all stakeholders. All the research projects strived to take into account the evolution of the local habitat, its identity, and the community's desire and capacity to respond to the most pressing needs while pursuing sustainable development goals.

Each of the book's studies employed a rigorous research methodology. The authors engaged multiple stakeholders through interviews, quantitative analyses, observations, and participatory meetings. The results offer a unique portrait of the current approaches to construction practices, land management, urban agriculture, and a variety of cultural practices. As a whole, the studies will hopefully stimulate broader discussions and reflections on action-oriented research and on development more generally. This could revolve around the following questions: 1) How can we, as researchers and practitioners, intervene effectively in the field? and 2) To what extent can the findings and experiences of these interventions be generalized? In other words, how do we build a knowledge bank that, while recognizing the particularity of the local context, also promotes the transferability of successful methods and approaches? And, how can methods and perspectives be applicable and transferable beyond the local context, and even beyond the domain of sustainable development? Such reflections could then result in an empirical and epistemological understanding of the interrelations of the methods presented in this book and, most importantly, of the significance of the vector that was unanimously presented as the core condition for development, namely, participation.

Participation: A key condition for success

For some time now, governments and multilateral agencies have made a point of praising the merits of good governance, participation, and decentralization. However, actual practices tend to be quite different, with governments usually remaining very centralized, leaving local areas with extremely little support. Projects aiming to regulate land ownership and other urban matters generally integrate participation at the implementation phase rather than the design phase of projects. Moreover, the design phase itself is often based on imported models that are rarely adapted to the climate, cultural practices, or needs of local households, particularly with regard to the deployment of productive practices. By contrast, community participation appears to be very strong in informal settings, at least based on the number of empowerment initiatives that have been reported in diverse publications. Many of these initiatives have been launched by women, with the aim of providing for their families and communities. However, on the whole, such empowerment projects engage very little with the government and are focused more on immediate subsistence measures than on the development of living environments at large.

All of the studies in the book engaged in an exploration of participatory approaches, founded on the sharing of knowledge among all stakeholders, the development of a collective vision, and the empowerment of communities to take charge of their territories. These approaches took account of the local cultures, however, without being limited thereto. The participation models were built on local culture and, in order to be inclusive of the most oppressed groups, broke with the patriarchal system and the traditional roles assigned to local associations and community leaders. In order to promote the involvement and motivation of communities, they also made use of the actors' skills and knowledge and the participative architectures that were taking root in each context. The studies illustrated the importance of incorporating such considerations in the design of participatory approaches, while also showing the difficulties associated with their implementation.

The studies by Pinard and Gagnon, both conducted in Malika, Senegal, underlined the importance of integrating these considerations into the design of participatory approaches, while also demonstrating the obstacles posed by poorly organized communities. As a sub-district with a great diversity of community workers and forms of aid, Malika has multiple forms of territorial governance, which often overlap, as well as land tenure problems, including the informality and non-transparency of land tenure management. This made the implementation of participatory processes, which are supposed to be inclusive of all institutions and people of a given neighbourhood, challenging. However, even under these demanding circumstances, the efforts towards participatory neighbourhood planning have proven to be convincing. In Pinard's action research, the participation of women, the community, and the various local actors was instrumental in finding appropriate solutions for improving the architectural layout and operations of a women's centre. The development of spatial designs, technical training, and measures to integrate agriculture into the compound, existing buildings, and new buildings was positive, as was the women's empowerment with regard to productive activities. In the case of Gagnon's action research, which concerned pig farming operations, involving the inhabitants in the project increased their participation and contributed to the implementation of adaptive solutions. The research of Ejigu, likewise demonstrating the importance of including communities, examined the planning stages of low-cost government housing programmes based on a case study of Addis Ababa, Ethiopia. The study highlighted the typical gap between the physical form of housing and the inhabitants' way of life. It moreover revealed that planners and decision-makers tend to be blinded by idealism, resulting in a neglect of the concrete environmental factors. Similarly, Tramhel's research emphasized participation by outlining the effectiveness of the asset-based community development approach in the integration of organic waste management into urban agriculture in Cagayan de Oro, Philippines. Here, the involvement of the community as early as the design phase of sustainable urban systems promoted capacity building among participants. All of these projects demonstrate the value of community engagement in design processes.

Linking concrete action with poverty reduction in urban areas

All the case studies were carried out as participatory action-research projects, which, by definition, seek to monitor and examine changes in participants' attitudes, perceptions, and practices throughout a project. In the spirit of grassroots fieldwork, the researchers engaged directly with the actors targeted by the interventions to develop ways of supporting productive activities and of ensuring healthy, equitable, and sustainable living environments through improvements to the design of the territory and to construction practices. In consultation with all key stakeholders, they also aimed to conceptualize and evaluate tools and approaches for ensuring interventions in the city on an ongoing basis. Table 10.1 (p. 168) lists the concrete sustainable actions for reducing poverty among the urban poor that were achieved with the projects from this book.

The concrete interventions in the various communities were highly participatory and served to identify stakes related to land tenure, urban services, and power relations. They also served to identify and strengthen local competencies and promote the building of community leadership. Here, the process often proved to be as important as the final outcome. Accordingly, the studies emphasized processes as well as the results. For example, in the case study by Pinard, the process of fostering women's participation in the project was just as important as the actual structural changes made to the women's centre. In the transfer of best practices from one locality to another, it is therefore important to state goals both in terms of processes and of expected results.

The studies showed the importance and challenge of balancing less-tangible benefits with concrete improvements in people's lives. The authors observed, for example, that the experts seemed somewhat challenged when tackling environmental matters with the population, as community members tended to focus on immediate problems and desires more readily than on problems that are less directly perceptible. Thus, immediate concrete results are critical for ensuring participants do not become disillusioned with urban interventions. They are also important for ensuring the buy-in of policy-makers, who often need to see to believe. In the following section I explore some of these more tangible achievements (see also Table 10.1 for an overview), before closing with general reflections on future prospects for urban sustainability.

In Chapter 1, we saw how the implementation of food-producing trees in productive systems in a public park constituted an effective contribution to the fight against food insecurity in the study neighbourhoods. The food production from these tree systems significantly promoted the involvement of the community in the maintenance and management of the trees, in turn favouring the longevity of these productive systems (Lafontaine-Messier). Chapter 2 featured a project on the links between polluted water used in urban agriculture and human health. It promoted community practices that minimize the risk of contamination at the farms, markets, and in households, among them the composting of organic manure, the treatment of wastewater before use, the disinfection of lettuce with chlorine prior to consumption, and avoidance of consuming groundwater as drinking water around the urban agriculture area (Ndiaye). In Chapter 3, the redesign of the Women's Centre of Malika promoted and incorporated productive activities into local architectural elements such as courtyards, and had an extremely positive impact on collective practices and initiatives. Since the conclusion of the project, the women have successfully taken charge of the activities initiated by the research team (Pinard). Chapter 4, the project on pig breeding in domestic settings, revealed new knowledge on the dynamic and practices of urban livestock production. This concerned, for example, the role of beliefs, representations, and social perceptions; the design of the Women's Centre; values concerning land, power relations, and mutual aid within the community (Gagnon). Chapter 5 presented the project on steering the demand and supply for low-income housing programmes, mainly through measures to build or buy less-crowded and better-quality housing. The resulting improvements included a reduction in the number of household accidents and removed the necessity for low-income groups to occupy land sites at high risk from floods, landslides, or other hazards (Kamruzzaman). In Chapter 6, the featured project concerned the relationship between residents' way of life and the spatial quality of the condominium compound they lived in. The project stimulated improvements to indoor spaces along with the creation of architectural elements that foster children's physical, mental, and social development (Ejigu). Chapter 7 presented the project on the analyses of mechanisms that promote the integration of certain informal drinking water services into the public sector. The project succeeded in providing technical expertise to the informal operator collectives for the installation of standpipes and the connection of households to the public drinking water distribution network (Katsongo). Chapter 8 presented the project on the integration of income-generating waste-reuse activities into the everyday lives of women and children living in a shelter on Koh Kred Island, Thailand. The researcher also engaged in efforts to turn this project into an ongoing, long-term programme (Guerra). Finally, Chapter 9 featured the implementation of the asset-based community development approach in the community in Cagayan de Oro, Philippines. Here, participants were engaged in a participatory design exercise to develop site plans for the integration of organic waste management into urban agriculture, resulting in increased local food production (Tramhel).

As a whole, all research activities contributed new knowledge on diverse dimensions of the transformation of living environments as well as on the participatory design process. The studies generated knowledge on current construction practices, the informal management of land, the morphology and characteristics of the built and natural environments, the organization of land leases, measures and designs for livestock breeding, social and political structures, and cultural practices. The results of these studies, together with an examination (still underway) of the Senegalese institutions and policies on urban planning and design, shed light on the actors and processes that participate in the creation and evolution of the living environments in 'rurban' zones, as well as on the stakes of participation, citizen involvement, and governance at the interface between traditional powers, official powers, and diverse emerging forms of citizen involvement.

It is my hope that all case studies in this book will serve to shed light on the links between sustainability and poverty reduction. As the combined problems of urbanization, environmental degradation, and poverty are becoming increasingly pressing, understanding these links is imperative. Poverty and environmental degradation form a vicious cycle. As demonstrated, low-income city dwellers live on the margins of urban life, without access to adequate environmental services and vulnerable to environmental burdens. The lack of basic amenities in turn contributes to further environmental degradation. Reversing this cycle and improving the health, quality of life, and security of the city as a whole therefore requires combating the marginalization of the city's low-income inhabitants. Despite the magnitude of this feat, low-income urban inhabitants have shown a strong drive to improve the quality of their environments and their lives. The research presented in this book sought to encourage and support this drive.

Working with vulnerable urban populations to improve their living environment is in the interests of everyone in the city – not only for the end result on the ground, but also for the 'community-lifting' effect that collaborative planning brings. A healthier environment, achieved mainly by improving income security, housing, and access to water for lower-income people, not only curbs public health risks linked to substandard living conditions but also reduces the risk of diseases spreading to other neighbourhoods. A healthier living environment offers better conditions for children to learn and thrive and for adults to be productive citizens and workers. Finally, a healthy living environment reduces public insecurity as a whole, locally and elsewhere in the city, as it spurs and attracts small businesses in addition to raising women's and youth's self-esteem (see the case studies by Guerra and Gagnon).

While it is nearly impossible to eliminate the pressures that impact low-income urban dwellers, the initiatives featured in this book demonstrate the feats that inhabitants of disadvantaged neighbourhoods, community organizations, and NGOs can accomplish to reduce these pressures, even with limited means. These achievements are greatly facilitated and enhanced when supported by local authorities and institutional stakeholders. We hope that this work has contributed to broadening the discourse and field of action on challenges facing researchers and practitioners working towards sustainable cities.

Table 10.1 Concrete actions from the book that can improve urban environments while reducing poverty

Name of authors and study location	Objectives of the research	Examples of concrete actions from the research	Direct and indirect effects on sustainability and poverty
Mariève Lafontaine-Messier Villa El Salvador, Lima, Peru	• Understanding of the advantages, drawbacks, constraints, and facilitating factors related to the development of productive spaces within public green spaces, and quantifying the economic impacts of these systems for the households, the community, and the municipality.	• Implementation of food-producing trees in productive systems in public parks.	• Allowed cultivation of large areas; made it possible to obtain yields that constitute effective contributions to the fight against food insecurity in the neighbourhoods being studied. • Created economic benefits and food production from these tree systems; significantly promoted the involvement of the community in the maintenance and management of the trees; in turn favouring the longevity of these productive systems and urban forestry projects in general.
Mamadou Ndiaye Pikine and Patte d'Oie, Dakar, Senegal	• Evaluating the impact of polluted irrigation water used in urban agriculture on the health of riparian populations.	• Examination of the microbial contamination of vegetables and groundwater caused by polluted water used in urban agriculture in the Dakar area. • Establishing links between polluted water used in urban agriculture and human health. • Promotion of community practices that minimize the risks of contamination at the farms, markets, and in the households, such as the composting of organic manure, the treatment of wastewater before use, the disinfection of lettuce with chlorine prior to consumption, and the avoidance of groundwater as drinking water around the urban agriculture area.	• Significantly reduced health burdens caused by water-borne infectious and parasitic diseases and some vector-borne diseases; reduced the rate of premature deaths. • For income earners, increased income from less time off work from illness or from taking care of sick family members; reduced expenditures on medication and health care. • Improved nutrition (e.g. less food lost to diarrhoea and intestinal worms). • Provided a set of scientific tools to assess and identify causes and to follow up with action in order to preserve human health.

Name of authors and study location	Objectives of the research	Examples of concrete actions from the research	Direct and indirect effects on sustainability and poverty
Émilie Pinard Malika, Dakar, Senegal	• Showing how architecture can become a catalyst for the participation of women in local governance and ecological practices; and ensuring the spread and dissemination of acquired skills regarding the reduction of environmental and sanitary degradation by applying an eco-systemic approach.	• Implementation of new constructions and architectural layouts that support productive activities (such as micro-gardening on roofs, dyeing, etc.); through workshops, promotion of the replication of such structural changes to homes and small public buildings.	• Generated new sources of food and income; experimented with new forms of productive activities; and trained other women and teenage girls so that these can adopt the acquired practices in their own place of habitation.
Jessica Gagnon Malika, Dakar, Senegal	• Improving pig breeders' living conditions and livestock breeding techniques and experimented with small-scale restructuring that reduces the sanitary and environmental risks to their households.	• Shaping of the architectural design of pig husbandry facilities in domestic environments. The interventions concerned: 1) the roofs and the management of the surrounding conditions; 2) floor coverings and the management of liquid pig manure; 3) the entry gate and work ergonomics; and 4) the distinction between the livestock production facility and the domestic space, and preventative measures.	• Raised support for livestock production and increased incomes. • Reduced the health and environmental problems generated by pig farms. • Reduced the contamination resulting from the interaction between people, their living environment, and livestock production, including the contaminants transmitted by livestock production. • Significantly reduced health burdens.

continued overleaf

Name of authors and study location	Objectives of the research	Examples of concrete actions from the research	Direct and indirect effects on sustainability and poverty
Mohamed Kamruzzaman Mirpur, Dhaka, Bangladesh	• Explaining how to steer the informal sector to best manage the demand for housing.	• Support of low-income groups to build or buy less-crowded and better-quality housing.	• Reduced the number of household accidents and removed the necessity for low-income groups to occupy land sites at high risk from floods, landslides, or other hazards. • Improved housing policies and increased the informal building capacity. • Scaled up housing production.
Alazar G. Ejigu Addis Ababa, Ethiopia	• Discussing how the interactive relationship between the residents' way of life and the spatial organization of condominium housing influences spatial use, and hence the functional and social performance of the housing estate; • Analysing the relationship between the way of life (also defined as 'lifestyle' in the study) of identified groups of residents and the spatial organization and spatial quality of the built condominiums.	• Demonstration of how different activities and social functions are supported, or impeded, by the nature of the physical environment and, conversely, how the spaces and facilities are used and transformed by dwellers to meet local demands. • Development of a more coherent operational view of architecture and planning as a social support instrument for the design and planning of cost-conscious, large-scale, multi-family housing environments.	• Stimulated the improvement of indoor spaces and the creation of benefits for children's physical, mental, and social development by offering better conditions for children to learn and for adults to be productive.

Name of authors and study location	Objectives of the research	Examples of concrete actions from the research	Direct and indirect effects on sustainability and poverty
Kamathe Katsongo Kisenso Kinshasa, Congo	• Examining eventual partnership modalities for managing drinking water in poor neighbourhoods of urban zones, with the objective of identifying and analysing mechanisms that can promote the insertion of some aspect of the informal sector into the public sector.	• Provision of technical expertise to the informal operator collectives for the installation of standpipes and the connection of households to the public drinking water distribution network.	• Reduced the time and physical effort needed to collect water, leaving more time for other activities. • Created a partnership between public actors, informal operator collectives, one outside partner, and users in order to supply drinking water to low-income neighbourhoods.
Diana Guerra Koh Kred, Thailand	• Understanding how collective action waste-reuse activities can contribute to local waste management, while at the same time increasing environmental quality and reducing poverty through income generation.	• Integration of income-generating waste-reuse activities into the everyday lives of communities. • Recovery of waste materials and incorporation thereof into traditional craft techniques to develop products.	• Helped the local community to maintain a long-term waste separation programme that integrates waste reuse as a daily activity and that generates income. • Improved self-esteem of the participants and personal skills with the perspective that, once outside the shelter, participants could generate their personal income by transforming waste into raw materials.
Jeannette M. E. Tramhel Cagayan de Oro, Philippines	• Verifying if the asset-based community development approach is well suited as a participatory urban-design tool for the development of resilient and sustainable cities, and if it is consistent with the basic principles of urban design.	• Engagement of the community in a participatory design exercise to develop site plans for the integration of organic waste management into urban agriculture.	• Improved community solutions for the use of waste as an agricultural input. • Increased local food production.

Index